Other Books by Giacomo Giammatteo

Non-Fiction:
No Mistakes Resumes,
Book I of **No Mistakes Careers**

Fiction:
Friendship & Honor Series:
Murder Takes Time
Murder Has Consequences

Blood Flows South Series:
A Bullet For Carlos: A Connie Gianelli Mystery
Finding Family, a Novella

Redemption Series:
Necessary Decisions: A Gino Cataldi Mystery

No Mistakes Interviews

How to Get the Job You Want

Giacomo Giammatteo

Inferno Publishing

Acknowledgments

The tough part of writing a book is not the writing, it's all the stuff that comes after that. I'll take credit for the writing. For the tough parts I am honor bound to thank the following:

My great copyeditor, Annette Lyon.

A fantastic graphic designer, Maria Zannini, for the book cover.

Christopher Fisher from The Editorial Department, for the amazing layout and formatting.

Katy Sozaeva for finding mistakes I didn't know were there.

And most importantly the army of beta readers who worked overtime to help me get this book into shape:

Rose, Bill K., Bill T., and Anthony Ferrante.

Special thanks to my grandsons, Joey and Dante, and to my granddaughter, Adalina for making my life brighter. And *grazie mille* to my niece, Emiliana, who kept me company and shared coffee with me on many late nights.

Lastly, to my wife, Mikki, who puts up with all of my nonsense. Without her, these books wouldn't be worth writing.

Ti amo con tutto il mio cuore.

Note to readers:

Throughout the book, I'll be referring to people as he or she, him or her, etc. I use these pronouns randomly, which in no way reflects one gender's appropriateness for any particular position.

No Mistakes Interviews

How to Get the Job You Want

Contents

Introduction

IF YOU READ MY BOOK on resume writing—*No Mistakes Resumes: Don't Get Caught in the Moat*—you learned that there was only one purpose for a resume—to get an interview. In this book, *No Mistakes Interviews: Don't Get Stuck on the Drawbridge,* you will learn that there is only one purpose for an interview—to secure a job offer, or the more likely scenario, another interview. The way we'll do that is by teaching you how to make it through the interview the *No Mistakes* way. Most of what we will cover consists of common-sense techniques, tried and true methods that have worked for a long, long time. The problem is that few people pay attention to the rules of interviewing, and you can't find these rules in many places, let alone in one place.

You won't find a lot of radical thinking in this book, nothing that any savvy person wouldn't pick up on her own. A couple of times, I advise pushing the envelope, but not drastically, just enough to grab the interview team's attention.

Why listen to me?

I've been a headhunter for more than 30 years, and I've interviewed thousands of people, both on the phone and in person. I've interviewed people in hundreds of cities and in all kinds of places—offices, hotels, airports, coffee shops, restaurants, golf courses, while playing poker, and in almost any number of other circumstances you can imagine. The one thing every interview had in common was that too many of the good candidates made horrible interview mistakes.

That is the primary reason I wrote this book—I got tired of seeing the best candidates *not* get the job offer. Yes, you heard me right. That adage is all too true:

The best candidate doesn't always get the job.

The fact of the matter is that the best candidate *quite often* doesn't get the job. And it's not for lack of trying; it's because they make *mistakes.*

Have you ever had an interview you thought you *nailed,* but then you waited, and waited, and waited for news, only to learn that you didn't get the job? Or maybe you got the second interview, but the result was the same—no job. Did you ever wonder what was going on while you waited? What took so long?

The most likely scenario is that the company was interviewing other candidates. If you weren't called back, it was because they found a better candidate—or at least they found a candidate they *thought* was better. Usually that happens because you didn't *sell* yourself during the first interview. You didn't do enough to convince them that you were the solution to their primary need or problem. And yes, quite often, the company has problems. If they have a job opening, there is a good chance they have a problem.

This book will teach you how to

- Identify the problem or primary need.

- Assess your skills as they relate to the problem/need.

- Sell yourself as the solution to the problem/need.

If you're ready to learn how to interview the *No Mistakes* way, let's get started. If you need to, put on your thick skin and arm yourself with a shield, because I'm going to be critical.

Are you ready? Okay, let's go get that job offer.

Title

IN MY FIRST BOOK OF THIS SERIES, I compared resume writing to storming a castle, and I even laid out a cast of characters you would meet in the book. Here they are again as a reminder.

Gatekeeper—First guardian of the castle. Defender of the moat. Also called Rose. She is the director of human resources for the castle. For those of you who may be wondering, I have a sister named Rose who happens to be a director of HR. Other than that, they have nothing in common. (Except physical appearance, manner of speech, and they both say "jackass" a lot. A *whole* lot).

Me—Narrator. Headhunter supreme. Always opinionated. Never wrong.

You—the candidate for the job, AKA the relentless one, slayer of dragons, savior of worlds, castle-storming knight-in-armor… and sometimes reduced to humble job seeker.

Wastebasket—This character has been replaced by a dumpster.

In this book you, will still be storming a castle, and still facing the same foes, including your arch nemesis, the gatekeeper, but the stakes are higher. If you screw up this time, you won't have boiling oil dumped on you, but you will have wasted a day or two of your life. And, of course, you won't get the job offer.

To avoid that, I'm going to offer sage advice. So don your suit of armor, or at least a suit, because we're going to siege a castle.

P.S. I said the characters in this book were essentially the same, but they're not. The wastebasket from the first book is now a dumpster. Back then, all we had to get rid of were resumes, but remember how I said the stakes were higher now? Well, in this book…let's just say there isn't enough room in the wastebasket for bodies.

Special note: At times you may think I come across a little sarcastic (or even a *lot* sarcastic) and that some of my examples and admonishments are harsh. I use this tone for one reason: to make a point. I want nothing more than for each and every one of you to be successful in getting a job offer. Following the examples in this book will help you achieve that goal.

Mistakes

"Never interrupt your enemy when he is making a mistake."
~ Napoleon Bonaparte

YOU CAN FIND MANY QUOTES about mistakes. Most deal with the philosophy of mistakes as a necessary part of life—a way to learn. I wholeheartedly agree. I believe that mistakes are the most important way to learn. But I also think there is a time and place for them. In other words, sometimes you can afford to make mistakes, and sometimes you can't.

Let me explain another way. If you were a tightrope walker, you could afford to make a mistake while practicing with a net beneath you. You *could not* afford a mistake while crossing the Niagara Falls Gorge with no net.

And you *cannot* afford to make a mistake during an interview.

This book will show you how to avoid the mistakes that plague many people during the interview process. Follow the advice, and you'll be a step ahead of the competition.

Note: If at any time while reading this book you begin to think, "This guy's a lunatic. Who cares about a few mistakes?"—if the thought even crosses your mind—think about this: a client told me that she could learn everything she needed to know about a candidate by the way they walked down the hall. Another client insisted he could do the same by how a candidate reacted to waiting in the lobby an extra fifteen minutes and by how the candidate treated the receptionist during that time.

Yeah. Scary, isn't it? The scariest part is that I'm not kidding—and neither were they.

PS: Neither one of them is a client anymore.

Phone Interview

MANY INTERVIEWS ARE PRECEDED by a phone screen. Those seem friendly, but don't be lulled into complacency. A phone interview is *not* a friendly chat; it's a process to eliminate you. You need to prepare for it just like you would for an on-site meeting.

A company conducting a phone interview with you could mean one of several things. Assuming you're an out-of-town candidate, this is standard procedure. It's a safeguard step in the interview process to further qualify you prior to spending the money to bring you in for an on-site visit.

If you're a local candidate, the call is of more concern. It typically means they aren't convinced from your resume and cover letter that you're worth their time. Sorry to be blunt, but it's true. This means you have work cut out for you, and you have to convince them to bring you in.

Phone Interview Preparation

Make a list of these points so you can have everything ready when they call.

- Prepare a quiet space, away from disturbances.
- Have a good phone connection. A landline is best.
- Have water or something else to drink at hand.

- Notepad and pen/pencil.

- Have your questions prepared and with you.

- Turn off call waiting.

- Tell your family/friends you'll be on an important call so they don't pick up the line or otherwise disturb you.

Let's Go Through These One At A Time

Prepare a quiet space, away from disturbances.

If you have animals, go somewhere they won't bother you or distract you while you're talking. Trust me, Murphy's Law always comes into play. You may have a dog who hasn't barked in two months, but something will happen to set the dog off while you're talking to the prospective employer.

Don't get me wrong. It's not that the employer will scratch you if they hear the dog bark, but it may distract *you*, making you nervous, and *that* could affect your interview. Why risk it? Get a place ready beforehand where you won't be bothered. I can't tell you how many times I've called candidates on scheduled interviews and had them answer the phone with kids crying in the background, or what sounded like a party going on. It didn't bother me, but I could tell the candidate was nervous.

Have a good phone connection. A landline is best.

Conduct the interview on a landline. Few cell phone connections are as clear or crisp as landlines, and you don't want the person on the other end struggling to understand what you say.

If you have a headset, and you *know* the sound is clear on *both* ends—use it. A good headset allows a more comfortable conversation, and it frees up your hands to take notes.

If you like to walk around while you talk, that's fine. Moving makes some people more animated, which comes through as enthusiasm in their voices. Just make sure you're not making noise while you walk.

Have water, or something to drink at hand.

You'll be doing a lot of talking, and talking makes your mouth dry, so make sure you have water.

Note pad and pen/pencil.

This is a no-brainer, but you'd be amazed how many people forget. I have often been interrupted with, "Hold on a minute while I get something to write with." (In case you're wondering—yes, that pisses me off.)

Have your questions prepared and with you.

Another no brainer. You have gone to the trouble of preparing questions, so make sure they're with you, and be sure to prepare them long before the call. Don't wait until ten minutes before the interview. I had one candidate ask me about the company's products and why they weren't doing well in the market. Great question—if he had gotten the product right. He was citing facts from the competitor, not our client.

It would also be great to practice the questions you anticipate from them. Remember, the questions you are asked on a phone interview will probably be different than ones they throw at you in a face-to-face session. If the position you're considering requires relocation, they *will,* or at least *should,* press you on whether you have discussed a move with your family and if relocation presents any problems.

Turn off call waiting.

There isn't much that is more irritating than to be conducting a phone interview and have it interrupted numerous times by incoming calls. Turning off call waiting is usually fairly simple. With AT&T U-Verse, you can do it online. You can likely do it through your voice mail. Check with your service provider. It's normally a simple process that takes a couple of minutes or less.

Tell your family/friends you'll be on an important call.

This one speaks for itself.

A Few Key Points About Phone Interviewing Etiquette.

Don't interrupt. Interrupting any conversation is never wise, but it's even more important not to during a phone interview, because it's often difficult to get back on track. If the person says something that sparks a thought…that's what the notepad is for. Jot down your thought and discuss it later. You'll have a chance to talk.

Don't ever discuss things like salary or benefits or relocation expenses over the phone. You should have all of the information you need prior to this call, and this is not the time or place to discuss it. This call is for them to determine whether they're interested in bringing you in for an interview. Don't do anything to deviate from that line of thinking.

Special Note About Phone Interviews

I have conducted more phone interviews (by far) than I have personal interviews. The number is certainly in the thousands. When you've done as many interviews on the phone as I have, you become adept at picking up on subtle clues and fluctuations in a person's voice. Things like hesitation, excitement, disappointment, enthusiasm, anger, frustration, and just about any other emotion you can imagine.

Many phone screens are conducted by nontechnical people, and I have seen some candidates—especially technical ones, like scientists and engineers—become frustrated and impatient when asked to explain for the second time about the technology involved with what they did. The people doing phone interviews are often *not* technical people, and they typically have strengths in the soft skills. They won't attribute any frustration they hear from you to your technical skills; instead, they'll likely read it as you being impatient.

So if the interviewer asks you a question, even if it's the same question for the third time, answer it with the same enthusiasm you did the first time.

A Note About Excitement And Enthusiasm

A recruiter's job is to fill a position for the clients. Recruiters work for the clients. Little frustrates a client more than going through the entire recruiting process only to have an offer rejected. So one of the recruiter's jobs is to evaluate how interested you are in the position/company, and what the likelihood is of you accepting an offer if it were to be extended. At the first sign of disinterest or trouble, you'll slip from the top rung of the ladder. You may not fall all of the way to the bottom, but you'll no longer be the favorite candidate.

"So what?" you say. "It's just the recruiter."

If you think the recruiter doesn't matter, you're wrong. The enthusiasm and excitement for specific candidates shows in the recruiter's voice when he/she presents the candidates to their clients. The clients then pick up on that, just like the recruiter did during the interview.

The Bottom Line

Maintain a positive attitude. Show enthusiasm and interest in the company and the position. Be excited! It will go a long way toward helping your cause.

You can turn a phone interview into a *win* if you stay focused on what matters. Always remember what the company's primary need or problem is, and focus on being the solution.

If you don't yet have a clear picture of what the company is looking for, this is a good time to discuss it. Ask the manager or human-resources representative for more detail on what is expected from the person in this position, and what the key requirements are. It's *critical* that you have a clear understanding of what the company wants prior to going in for an on-site interview.

Travel Arrangements

SINCE YOU JUST FINISHED your phone interview, we're taking a detour to discuss travel arrangements. If you will never be concerned with traveling to an interview, you can skip this chapter.

After you completed the phone screen, they probably told you that someone would be in touch, or they might have even told you they want you to come in for an interview. Either way, let's assume you're going for an on-site visit and that you've been contacted about travel arrangements.

The Three P's Rule

Polite: It goes without saying that you should be polite. Practice being polite with everyone, but especially in cases like this. You never know who you're dealing with. I had a candidate who was, for lack of a better description, a pain in the ass. He was inflexible, picky, and bordered on obnoxious to the lady who was helping him with arrangements. What he didn't know was that she was good friends with the hiring manager. He became so difficult that she told the manager about it, and they canceled the interview.

Precise: Try to be precise in all communication, but when dealing with schedules, meetings, flights, and anything else involving time, precision is imperative. Whether you're communicating by email or phone, when you mention a time, include the time zone.

Instead of saying you'd prefer to leave on a flight "after 4:00 PM," say, "after 4:00 PM Central time."

Instead of "Wednesday at 8:00 is good for me." How about "Wednesday, the 14th at 8:00 AM Central will work great."

Practice being precise, and you'll save both the company and yourself a lot of time, and possible miscommunication.

Professional: If there is one rule that is *always* mandatory, it's to be professional. Make professionalism part of your life, whether you're interviewing or not, but especially *while* you're interviewing. It seems that people lose all control when dealing with travel arrangements.

Here are some basic rules you should abide by.

- Don't ask for upgraded seats or to fly first class.
- Don't ask for extra nights in the hotel or to bring your spouse and/or children.
- Don't ask for a different hotel or a different airline.
- Don't ask for a special rental car.
- Don't ask for a rental car if they offer a taxi or a shuttle.
- Don't ask for a taxi if they offer a shuttle.

During my 30 years as a headhunter, I have seen many requests from candidates. Most of them are reasonable, but some are damn rude. If you're invited to an interview and you have special requests after hearing the travel arrangements, ask your headhunter about them. If you're not dealing with a headhunter, make certain your request is reasonable and offer to pay for the extra accommodation yourself.

Scenario 1: You're flying to San Francisco for an interview on Friday, and they have you flying back out Friday night. You think, *My spouse would love to go. We could spend the weekend.*

Options: Explain to whomever you're dealing with that you're serious about the position and that your spouse would like to come along so he/she could explore the area while you interview. You'd also like an extra night (or two) in the hotel.

What's acceptable: Tell them *up front* that you're willing to pay for the additional cost, and that you would simply like the convenience of seats next to each other on the plane and the same room at the hotel.

What's not acceptable: Anything else.

If the company wants to pay for your spouse's airfare and any extra night, they'll offer to. If they see you as the front-running candidate for the job, they may elect to pay the extra costs. If not, they'll probably take you up on your offer to pay. Either way, their response should tell you something.

Scenario 2: You're flying to the same company in San Francisco from Boston. It's a six-hour flight, and they have you flying coach in a window seat. You hate window seats.

What's acceptable: Tell who you're dealing with that you have a frequent-flyer program on this airline and would like to use rewards to upgrade to first class, or to a better seat. Offer to pay for the upgrade if you don't have the rewards.

What's not acceptable: Anything else.

If you ask for an upgrade, especially on their nickel, you risk the chance they'll think you are a prima donna, and that you'll want to fly first class all the time. Some companies go for that; most don't.

Note: I had one situation where the candidate lived about 200 miles from the other company. They were going to fly him in on a Thursday night for a Friday-morning interview and then fly him back out on Friday evening. He asked me if he could drive up with his family and stay two extra nights in the hotel so they could look around the area. He had already checked, and the money the company would save on the flight would more than pay for the hotel accommodations. I thought this was a reasonable request and asked the hiring manager, who ended up agreeing to the hotel and paying for the man's driving expenses as well.

One thing to remember is that you are not the only person the company is interviewing for the job. They are likely flying in three or four people minimum. It would get very expensive to make extra accommodations for everyone.

To put this in perspective, think of a wedding. You don't ask to bring extra guests if they're not on the invitation, do you?

The Interview

OKAY, YOU ARE FINALLY at the interview stage. You've put together a perfect resume, survived the screening process, and received an invitation for an interview. Now the fun starts.

If you read the last book *No Mistakes Resumes*, you'll know how damn hard you worked to get this interview. If you didn't read it, trust me; you worked damn hard to get here.

Now the Competition Starts

I know what you're thinking. *Competition?* Don't kid yourself. This *is* a competition. If you're not competing against other candidates, you're competing against the job specs. If you're lucky, all you have to do is beat the person who had the job before. In the worst-case scenario, you'll be competing with the imaginary person the interview team has in their heads. I'll give you a clue as to who that is: He wears a red and blue suit with a big S on it.

Remember, most interviewers are busy, they *don't* want to be interviewing you, and they certainly don't want to discuss your interview later. The only ones who really want to see you are the HR representative and the hiring manager. So if you want this job, you'd better do a damn good job of selling yourself.

I can help you with that, but we have to get down to the basics.

That means preparing for the interview the *No Mistakes* way. There are four basic parts to a successful interview, and one of the most important is preparation.

Before you start preparing, make sure you understand the company's *primary need.* Being able to identify this is one of *the most important* parts of the interview process.

Identify the Primary Need

ONCE YOU UNDERSTAND THE COMPANY'S primary need, you should focus your interview on solving that problem or addressing that need.

Note: When I refer to the *primary need* or the *need*, I don't mean necessarily one single item. The need could be two or three things, but seldom more than that. I may also refer to it as the *problem*. Some positions are open because the company has a problem. Other times, it's simply due to growth or succession planning. For example, a grocery store is hiring a new cashier. I would categorize that as *filling a need*, although it could just as easily be cited as a *problem*. After all, if the need goes unfilled, the checkout lines will get longer, and customers will be unhappy.

An argument could be made that all open positions are *problems* in one sense or the other. Often it's a matter of semantics. But for the sake of argument, openings for hiring fresh college grads, filling positions to accommodate forecasted growth, and similar circumstances, we'll refer to as *primary needs* as opposed to *problems*. Throughout this book I'll use the terms *primary need* or *need* and *problem* interchangeably.

Technically this section should be part of *preparation*, but identifying the need is so important that it deserves to be separate.

This section will also be one of the shortest chapters, because everything you need to know about this part of the book, you should already know. If you don't know what the company needs, talk to your HR representative or recruiter to find out *exactly* what the company's primary need is for this position.

I said this section was important. I think it is *the* most important thing for you to know. If you do nothing else before going to the interview, find out what the company's primary need is.

Knowing What the Company Wants

Job descriptions tend to list far too many things as requirements and duties. All that does is confuse the issue and dilute the effect of what's really important. To be successful in getting an offer, focus on the one or two things that are really important. I know I keep saying "the one or two things," and a lot of times there may be many more than that, but in most cases you will find *one single thing so* important that if someone can show the company that they can fix the problem or address the need, they'll get the job offer.

You should have gathered this information before you put your resume together, but in case you didn't, let's walk through how to get it. Here are a few sources to get this information.

- Headhunter
- Representative from the company
- Job description
- Internal contacts at company
- Contacts who used to work at company

The first thing you need to know is that you can't rely on *any* of these sources, which is why you need to get busy and take advantage of all of them.

Headhunter: You *may* have a headhunter who is intimately familiar with the company and the hiring manager, one who knows everything the company needs and the kind of people they like. But you may also have a headhunter who just got this assignment the week before and knows nothing about the company, the manager, or even the job. So pick their brain, take notes, but don't count on what they tell you to be gospel, because some of them try to bullshit you so they don't look bad.

Representative from the company: Things are no different when dealing with a company representative. He/she may be new, may not know the manager well, may have just been assigned to recruit for this department…the list goes on and on. An exception to this rule is if you're dealing directly with the hiring manager; we'll hope *they* have a good idea of what they want. But even then, don't trust only this source. The manager may not want to share his/her problems with you at this stage of the game. Remember, you're only one of several candidates they'll be talking to. He/she may be waiting to narrow it down before revealing their dirty laundry.

Job description: This falls somewhere between company rep and hiring manager as far as reliability. It *should* be filled with information you can use, but it may also be an old, reworked description that should have been updated but wasn't. (Look for dates on the job description. Sometimes they're left on from earlier versions. I have been sent job descriptions written three years before.) In any case, the description should list several different skills the job requires:

- Technical skills, such as programming in C++, or experience with a particular manufacturing system, or knowledge of FDA submissions for medical devices.

- Functional skills, such as strong organizational ability, or excellent verbal and written communication.

Write down the three most important challenges/duties mentioned in the job description. Next to them, write the top requirements. Now try to figure out the single most important requirement. For the time being, focus on that as the target, but remember that will be an ongoing, ever-changing process. As the interview progresses and you learn more about the job/company, what you thought was the top requirement may change. Be prepared to think on your feet and adapt your responses.

Once you have what you feel are the three key requirements of the job and the three main needs/problems they need solved, you are prepared to start the rest of the process. The easy part is done. Now all you have to do is organize your notes. You'll need them for the preparation part.

Contacts—current and past: If you have contacts at the company, use them. If you can find contacts you trust who used to work at the company, they can be your most valuable source. Pull out all stops to find a source like this.

Note: You may not think the requirements for this job are right, but regardless, address them anyway; those requirements are what the company feels they need for a person to be successful in this position.

Because this is so important, I'm saying it again: Identifying the company's primary need is *the most important* thing you can do to ensure success.

Preparation

THE PREPARATION SECTION is the longest part of this book, and rightfully so. In real life, that's how most things are. Think of the poor gymnast who trains all her life for a few minutes at the Olympics, or the actors/actresses who rehearse for months for a few minutes of screen time. It's even reflected in everyday things like cooking. It takes my wife almost two days to make her lasagna, but once she puts it on the table, it's devoured within minutes.

The interview is no different. Doing it right takes a lot of preparation. By comparison, it takes far less time than all the other examples I gave, but getting fully prepared takes work.

This is a job change, people! Spend time on it. Most people spend less time researching a potential new employer than they do a TV or a new car purchase.

I said that preparation was one of the most important parts of this process, and here's why. To become good at anything, you have to practice. Most people don't get to practice interviewing because they're employed, not looking for a job. In an odd twist on fate, the best interviewers usually turn out to be the *naturals*, those people who have a knack for performing on the spot, thinking on their feet, and adapting to any situation. There is even a saying that "The best *interviewee* is the one who gets the job."

That saying is *all too true.*

Other than the naturals, the second best group of people who do well in interviews are the ones who have had the most practice—in other words, the people who are always looking for a job. They may not be the best people for the jobs, but they often get them because they understand how to interview.

That was a longwinded way of getting to the point, but we've finally arrived. This is why you need to prepare: if you've had a stable career, you probably haven't had interviewing practice.

When it comes to preparation, start with company research. Everything else builds off that.

Company Research

I DON'T KNOW WHY YOU'RE LOOKING for a job. You could have many reasons: you're laid off, pissed off, your spouse got a new job and you have to move, you don't like where you live, don't like where you work…The potential list is endless, but regardless of the reason, we will presume that you want to join a company with the goal of staying for a while. That means you want to find a company that matches your needs. That topic alone could be another book, but we'll assume you know what your needs are. Now all you have to do is see if the company you are interviewing with can meet those needs. That process begins with the company research.

How Much Do You Know About the Company?

- What products do they make, or what services do they offer?
- What is their position in the market?
- What is their reputation?
- Who runs the company and what is their philosophy?
- What is the employee turnover rate?

- Are the employees happy?
- What is the public's view of the company and their products/services?

These and a thousand other questions *should* be going through your mind. If you're an engineer driven by designing the best product possible, you don't want to join a company known for rushing products to market with a quality-be-damned attitude. Suppose you're an HR person with the goal of creating a phenomenal environment for the employees, but the company you're about to interview with has the highest turnover in the industry. Not a good fit unless they're bringing you in to change it.

Where to Find the Information?

Fortunately, we have the Internet. I said this would be hard work, but it isn't, not compared to pre-Internet days. So open up a browser and pull up your favorite search engine. It's time to get started.

The easiest and most logical, place to start is the company's website. A website is a wealth of information for anyone preparing for an interview. Let's start with the mundane things, like contact information. While you're there, add the company information to your smartphone if you have one, or at least write down or copy the phone number for the location you'll be visiting. Then find the address and driving directions.

Also check out the media section and look at press releases.

- Has the company made any recent announcements?
- Have they had any recalls?
- Have any new products launched?
- When was their last announcement?

You can learn a lot from this section, so don't ignore it.

You will, of course, want to visit the product/services section. This is the meat. You want to see what they're doing, what's new, and perhaps note any technical details of the products.

Management team—this is one of the most important aspects of your research. Take a good look and jot down notes.

This is just one stop for management team research. We'll get to the rest later.

Now go to glassdoor.com and do more research. Glassdoor is a great site for getting a perspective from past employees. You can often find information on salaries, jobs, interviews, and general company gossip. The insight into the interviews can be helpful if there's enough information listed. You can't necessarily trust all of the gossip, but if nothing else, the information can give you a good base with which to do further research.

When you finish with Glassdoor, go back to the search engine and type in "company name AND rumors." Many sites run rumor mills on companies or industry segments. You'll have to sift through the information to see what you think is real, but doing such a search is often worth it. When investigating a potential client, I found a site where no less than 20 or 30 people were complaining about the company's continually changing policies on compensation for sales reps—too many complaints to ignore. Not a good thing.

What to Do with the Information?

Okay, so you've done all this work. What for?

You'll use some of this information for the questions you'll ask the interview team. Suppose the company has been in business for seven years but has yet to release a product. If it were me, I'd be asking a lot of questions about that. The research you did is also good for determining how to answer questions or what you'll use for a presentation, assuming one is required.

Now that you've finished doing company research, let's move on to employee research.

Employee Research

THIS IS DEFINITELY A SECTION you don't want to skip. By now you've probably received your itinerary and a list of who will be on the interview team, including their titles. If you haven't been provided this information, contact your headhunter, or whomever you're dealing with at the company, and ask for a copy. You need to know who you'll be meeting.

Remember, in the *No Mistakes Resumes* book, I said the resume is not about you; it's about the company. But the interview is a two-way street.

You'll see a lot of advice that contradicts what I say,* advice insisting that the interview is still all about the hiring company. I disagree. I believe you need to show the company early on that you're interested and can solve their problems, but also that you're an active and integral part of this process. In fact, I firmly believe that by taking this approach you'll impress the hiring company even more. You've entered a new phase, and it's not just about them anymore. Now we're talking a marriage, and as you know that's a...

Two-way Street

Yes, a two-way street. That means you need to know as much about them as they know about you. Ever see a bad marriage?

Of course you have. Marriages fail for a lot of reasons. People change. Beliefs change. Mistakes are made. But not all marriages go sour because of things that happen *after* the marriage; sometimes it's because not enough was done during the preparation phase. Sometimes people let a physical attraction race out of control—right into a marriage.

This same scenario happens every day, about a million times a day, with jobs. Companies hire people and people accept offers they have no business accepting. People take jobs and join companies that fail to match their career goals.

One big step in avoiding that is to do good research before the interview. Earlier I had you gather the names listed on the company website, and that was for one reason—to make sure you had the proper name and title. You'll need to dig deeper than the website to find anything of value *about* the people you'll be interviewing with. Fortunately, social media, particularly LinkedIn, makes a difficult job easy.

Doing the Research

If you aren't on LinkedIn, stop what you're doing and join. You can say all you want about social media, but if you're looking for a job, the only social media that truly matters is LinkedIn. To give you an idea of the networking power there, look at this example from my own LinkedIn page:

- Your LinkedIn network: 15,111 connections link you to 26,145,724+ professionals.

Yes, you read that right. My 15,000+ connections link me to more than 26 *million* professionals. That's a lot of people. Even if you don't want to spend the time to build your social network, at least hook up with a few people who have a lot of connections; that will expand your reach greatly. For more information on how to use LinkedIn, go to the site and search for LinkedIn experts. You should be able to find a list of people far more knowledgeable than I am.

Back to the research.

Common Ground

This segment of the research has two segments. Using LinkedIn, search for people currently working at the company. If it's a large company, narrow it down by location and even by department. Your goal is to find common ground with the interview team. If the director of sales is on the schedule, pull up her profile and see where she worked before. Perhaps you know someone at one of those companies. If so, ask them what she was like to work with. Gather any other information that may give you an advantage. If the person you know is an acquaintance whose name can be brought up comfortably during the interview, do so; it may help. Not much is better than sharing common ground.

Even if you don't find any connections you can use, make a copy of the person's profile and keep it with the rest of your research. It will be important when it comes time to put together questions to ask. You're almost done this part of the research, but before you leave the page, let's find out where they hide their…

Dirty Laundry

This sounds like a crude thing to discuss, but it's important. This is your career, remember? You can't let an aversion to snooping stop you from making the right decision. Let's change the search settings on this page to find former employees. We'll start with who had this job before.

Example: if you're interviewing for a manager of customer service position, go to the advanced search and put "customer service manager" in the box for the title. In the option below that, choose "past not current." Then type in the company name, and again choose "past not current," in the box below "company." You should pull up a list of people who previously held this position or at least who have worked in the department.

Now you have several options. You may find common ground with the person: groups you are both members of; contacts you have in common; or previous employers, even if your time there didn't overlap. If you feel bold enough, make contact and ask them about the company, job, boss, why they left, etc. At the very least, you'll have a profile of someone who previously had the position, and you can ask questions based on that.

Name Pronunciation

Before we quit, let's talk about name pronunciation. This seems like a silly thing, but knowing how to pronounce an interviewer's name gives you an edge. Once you have the names of the interview team, ask your contact at the company, or the headhunter, how to pronounce each name. Write them down phonetically and keep the note with you. Practice saying the names a few times. Getting the pronunciation right makes a huge impression, especially with difficult names. Get a person's name right, and you start off one step ahead of the competition, or at the very least on even ground. Get a person's name wrong, and you...well, you know what they say about first impressions.

Okay, that was easy. Let's move on to the questions.

*I've seen a lot of advice saying that at the interview stage the focus is still all on the company, not you. I don't agree. Once the company invites you for an interview, it becomes a two-way street, as far as I'm concerned. And if your attitude reflects that thinking, it can actually be an advantage. Most good managers I know want to be challenged. They want someone unafraid to push the envelope. If you come across too similar to every other candidate, you're...well...like every other candidate. My advice is to go for it. Ask them the same kind of tough questions they ask you. Make them *show you* that their company is where you want to work, and that their job is the challenge you've been looking for. Make the hiring manager show you she/he is the kind of boss you'd like to work for.

Personal Research

IF YOU NEVER INTEND TO RELOCATE, feel free to skip this section. Personal research is an important part of the job-seeking process, but one that will have little bearing on the actual interview, because you shouldn't bring any of it up, at least, not at the first interview. This is all about gathering information you will need to make clear decisions. I'm putting this with the interview preparation, but it should have been done long before this.

Data

There is a lot to consider when faced with a relocation.

Taxes: If you're moving to a new state, does it have an individual income tax? Seven states don't: Alaska, Florida, Nevada, South Dakota, Texas, Washington, and Wyoming. Taxes can have a big negative influence on your income if you're moving from Texas (which has no income tax) to California (which has one of the highest income taxes). But you also need to check sales taxes, real estate taxes, corporation, and local taxes, especially if you or your spouse/partner have a side business.

Cost of housing: I separated cost of housing from cost of living because it has so much impact on cash flow. In the years I've been headhunting, housing has been the primary reason why most families won't relocate, and the biggest stumbling block when it comes to compensation negotiations. (More on that later.) To give you an example: Several cost-of-living comparison sites listed San Francisco as being about 125-135% more expensive to live in than Houston. But the cost of housing was 3.5–4.5 times as much. A house in Houston that costs $300,000 would cost you between $1,050,000 and $1,350,000 in San Francisco. That is a number a lot of people couldn't live with. It would be a deal breaker for many people.*

I did a *lot* of recruiting for clients in the bay area during the past 30 years; in fact, most of my business has been there. I got used to screening people out based on this one factor alone. I questioned them in detail about their house, its value, and if they'd be willing to sacrifice on housing. In many instances, they might have been going from a house with 3,500 square feet to one with 2,200 square feet. That decision had to be made before we ever set up an interview. I tried to make sure they made the decision before they sent a resume. The last thing I wanted was to waste my client's time. Or mine.

Cost of living: This is a factor, but not nearly as big of a factor as housing. Plenty of online sites do cost-of-living comparisons. Find sites that separate housing from other costs, and that give you a breakdown so you can determine relevance. Many sites break down expenses by utilities, gasoline, cost of cars, movies, food, etc.

Bottom Line

The point of this section is to remind you that if you haven't done this work yet, get on it now. The last thing you want to do is move ahead with an interview only to find out that there is no way you'd make the move. Do that, and you'll piss off the recruiter *and* the company. Those are bridges you don't want to burn.

*This subject could take almost an entire book by itself. Doing research on cost of living, cost of housing, and comparing the differences is a time-consuming job. Doing it properly will take many hours, and it requires a financial acumen you may not have. State income taxes, state and federal income tax deductions, sales tax, real estate taxes, interest rates, bridge loans, sign-on bonuses (and the tax implications), equity appreciation, and other things all have to be considered. This is an area you want to spend time on. I have salvaged numerous deals because the people weren't looking at the data right. If you want the job, do this part right. Look at it with an eye toward making it work. There is almost always a way to make it happen.

What Are They Going to Ask Me?

THAT'S A GOOD QUESTION, and one you should be asking your-self. It's not as big a mystery as you may think. Most companies adhere to a fairly typical process when it comes to interviewing. I know you may have heard crazy scenarios, like interviewers who ask riddles, or who ask you ridiculous life-and-death questions. But for the most part, companies rely on trusted methods to get the information they want, and those methods almost always consist of a few standard questions, combined with position-specific questions. Let's look at some of the standard ones.

- Why did you leave your job? (Or why would you consider leaving your job?)

- Why are you interested in this job/company? (Or why do you want to work for us?)

- What are your weaknesses? (No matter how they phrase it, this question will almost certainly be part of the interview.)

Besides these standards, there will be specific questions, and it's easy to figure out what they may be. Take a look at the job description and tear it apart. All of the questions should be there. Most companies use a behavioral-based interviewing system based on the belief that past behavior and performance will predict future behavior and performance. We can argue at another time whether or not that's the best method, but since the companies you're likely to be interviewing with will probably use it, you'll need to know how to deal with these questions.

Behavioral-based questions can usually be recognized by how they start. "Tell me about a time…" or "Describe a situation…"

The questions are left open-ended because the interviewer wants you to relate a story to them. They don't want a one- or two-sentence answer. Be prepared when the company asks questions like, "Tell me about a time when you had to deal with a problem employee and how you resolved that conflict," or, "Tell me about a time when you experienced conflict with a coworker."

Full Alert

When the interviewer starts to ask behavior-based questions, go on full alert, because these may be the most important questions of the interview. There is an endless list of questions they could ask, so if they're asking about conflict with a co-worker, or resolving conflict with employees, there's a good chance similar problems exist with this job or in that department. How you answer will have a major impact on their decision regarding whom to hire.

Your answer must deal with the question in a story-based way and should have three parts. The first part states the problem, the middle talks about the action you performed, and the ending is where you tell the results. Tell the story concisely and in a fluid manner, but without it sounding rehearsed.

Here's an example of what a response may sound like to this question: "Tell me about a time when you had to deal with a problem employee and how you resolved that conflict."

> "We were implementing a new quality system, and it changed the way we did a lot of things in our department. An employee who had been a consistent performer suddenly was below par, and worse, had become disruptive.

"I had a sit-down with him and, after a few talks, he opened up about how he had been struggling with the new system. I realized there might be others in the same situation, so I had face-to-face meetings with everyone in the department and identified three people who felt they needed help. I got approval from my boss, and we provided some *retooling*, which consisted of off-site training, followed by assigning a mentor to each person from the group.

"The result was that we not only fixed the issue with that first employee, but I feel we prevented possible problems with a couple of others. The situation taught me a lesson, too. I hadn't been paying enough attention to how the department was adjusting to the new system, probably because I was adjusting to it myself. I learned that some people need more help and more time adjusting to change."

This was a good response. The person showed empathy and admitted it was partly his fault, and he closed his response by showing that he learned from the experience. That's the kind of person I'd want on my team.

Other Questions

You won't know every question they'll ask you, but you can anticipate the types of questions they'll ask based on the job description. If it's a job in quality control requiring meticulous work, they'll ask questions that will bring out your attention to detail. If the job involves advertising, the questions may be geared more toward creativity and artistic areas, combined with good communication skills. The key to preparing your answers lies in knowing your background. What I mean by that is understanding and being able to communicate concisely what your skills are, what your accomplishments are, and how they relate to the job description.

Pull out your resume and the job description and go through notes you have from the headhunter or the HR representative, and any notes you took from the phone interview. Go through every duty and responsibility of the job description and come up with support for why you are the right candidate, even if the accomplishments to justify that aren't on your resume. This will help you show that you're the person for the job.

And More Questions

Aside from the specific questions, another one likely to come up is, "Tell me about your greatest accomplishment."

When you answer this question, make sure the response is relevant to the job. The way to prepare for this question is to make note of all your major accomplishments and then make sure you practice and have a clear idea of how to communicate not only *what* you did, but *how* you did it. That is the most important thing to remember in the interview process—your answer has little to do with *what* and everything to do with *how*.

If you wrote a good resume—and I'm assuming you did, because you got the interview—the company already knows *what* you did. Now they want to understand *how* you did it. They want to see who helped you, if it was good fortune or good planning, and most important of all, whether you can duplicate that success at their company, in this position, with the team they have.

One more thing: You can't prepare for every question they'll ask you, and sometimes one of the interviewers may throw you a surprise question. If you find yourself facing a question you don't know the answer to, it's all right to simply say, "I don't know," but always follow that up with, "but I'll find out for you," and then give them a time when you'll get back to them. That's not only an acceptable response, it's one I strongly recommend. We'll discuss this more later.

Now that you know what you need to do to prepare for the interview, let's practice what you'll say.

Note: Be prepared to think on your feet and change your practiced spiel at any time. Why? Because you can't count on the interview team to be prepared. The HR person will be prepared, and the hiring manager will be prepared, but don't count on the rest of the team. Many of them may be winging it, which means you could have any kind of question thrown at you, or they may discuss who won the most recent sporting event for the local area. So be sure to *listen* to the questions and answer appropriately.

Practice Makes Perfect

WERE YOU EVER IN a school play?

Ever give a speech in front of a large crowd?

Perform in a movie?

Been a guest on a radio show?

Ever tightrope walk?

No? Okay, remember *anything* that you ever did for the first time. How about riding a bike? You weren't quite as good at it the first, second, or even third time as you were later. No matter what you do or what you try, *practice makes perfect*. We know it's true because that's where the damn saying came from.

Interviewing Is No different.

The ideal situation is to practice with someone, but if that's not possible, practice alone, talking out loud. Regardless of what you think, hearing your own voice makes a difference. One of the best ways to practice is speak into a tape recorder and then listen to yourself. But listen to yourself later, not right away. If you do it right after the practice, you're still hearing the voice in your head, the one that sounded great. But a few hours later or the next day, you'll hear the real you, and you may be surprised at how bad you sound. (Think about how you *think* you sound when you sing along with a tune, and how you *really* sound.)

Practice until you're comfortable with your responses. That's how to build confidence. And confidence is a powerful weapon in an interview. Don't underestimate it.

Confident or Conceited?

While you want to be confident, you want to avoid being perfect. You don't want to sound rehearsed, and you definitely don't want to come off as cocky or arrogant or conceited. There is a fine line between confident and conceited; the dictionary definitions are almost interchangeable.

Conceited:

1. Having an excessively favorable opinion of one's abilities, appearance, etc.

Confident:

1. Sure of oneself; having no uncertainty about one's own abilities, correctness, successfulness, etc.

2. Excessively bold; presumptuous.

As you can see from these definitions, the slightest shift can make you appear conceited instead of confident. One way to avoid being perceived as conceited or arrogant is to be judicious in how you use the word "I."

Remember, on resumes and in interviews, the word *I* is no good. I'm sure you've heard of the old saying, "There is no I in *team.*"

I have a different saying: "There are two I's in *idiot* and two in *egotistical.*"

This problem was easy to fix on the resume; we simply left out the first-person pronouns—I, we, me—and let them be understood. So instead of writing, "I increased sales by 30%..." you wrote, "Increased sales by 30%..." In an interview, it's not that easy.

There Is a Fine Line Between *I* and **We**

Every company I know wants a team player—but they also want high-performers. Sometimes those two traits don't exist in the same person. Because of this, companies are always on the lookout for the ones who may not fit with their culture. To avoid being categorized as a lone wolf, be conscious of the pronouns you use. During an interview, replace *I* with *we*, except in a few key places.

Let's assume the question is, "Tell me about a time when a project was running behind schedule, and what you did to correct it."

Instead of saying, "I did this, or I did that," start with *we*.

"We had a new product that *absolutely* had to be launched before Christmas, but when I got the assignment, we were already behind by two months. After consulting with the team, I decided to take a slightly different approach to supplier management."

Analysis

Notice how in this response, the candidate used *we* to show group ownership of the product and responsibility for launching it. Then he switched to *I* to show that he got the assignment, in other words, it was *his* responsibility, his ass on the line. The end of that sentence switches back to *we*, where the project was behind by two months. The next sentence clearly shows that it was his decision to take a new approach, but only after consulting with the team, so he is sharing credit, but making it clear that he was in charge.

I'm not showing the last part here for confidentiality reasons, but the candidate closed his response with specifics on exactly what he did in the supplier management area and showed how it resolved their problem. The product was launched two days ahead of schedule, though it ended up being 3% over budget.

Bottom Line

If you take that same response and use *we* in all instances, it sounds fake. If you do the reverse, using *I* in every case, it sounds egotistical. Only when you mix them up does it come off as genuine.

Some people suggest using *I* consistently in all responses; others advise the opposite, suggesting you use *we*. I think a good balance is best, knowing when to use *I* and when to use *we*. Like everything else in the interview, it's going to be your call, but I'd give this some thought and even practice in front of others to get their opinions.

What Should I Ask Them?

Sources for Questions

Most of your questions should focus on the company and the position. But that doesn't mean you can't dig deeper. Depending on the situation, you should have plenty of time to probe into your potential boss' background, management style, and why the job is open. So where do you find the questions?

In the last chapter, we discussed how to prepare for the company digging deeper into your background. Now it's time to give *you* the shovel. As I said before—contrary to what many believe—an interview is a two-way street. It's no longer *just* about the company. They've taken your time and brought you in for an interview. You owe it to yourself, and to *them*, to dig deeper and find out if you're really interested in working for them.

Job Description

This should be your primary source for the questions you ask about the position. It's also what the company will use to ask their questions, at least many of the detailed technical questions.

- Find the top three requirements. If they aren't listed, or aren't obvious from the description, make note of what you *think* they are, and then ask others for clarification.

- If you're working with a recruiter, he/she should know the top three requirements. If they don't know, they can easily find out from the hiring manager or HR representative.

- If you have any contacts inside the company, ask them.

- If you don't have contacts inside the company, and you're not dealing with a headhunter, ask your contact at the company.

Company Research

Go back through your preparation. When you researched the company, I'm sure you found things that piqued your curiosity—maybe a press release on the website mentioned a Series B round of funding. That kind of thing spurs questions.

- How much money did they raise?

- How long will that money last?

- What's the burn rate?

- What's the exit strategy?

If you discovered a recent product recall, that should definitely lead to questions.

- What happened?

- What did you do to correct the problem?

- How much did the recall damage the company's reputation, and what are you doing to repair that?

Employee Research

Mirror questions—What you want to do is use *mirror* questions to get more information. [We'll go into that more in a few chapters.]

Personal questions—During your employee research, you should have gathered information on the interview team. During the interview, you can put that information to good use by asking questions to gain valuable insight into the company and how it works.

Example questions:

- I noticed you came from a large company, like I do. How long did it take to adjust to working in a start-up environment, and what did you find most difficult to adjust to?

- I see that most of the top management team came from one company. Does that present a problem with others "fitting in"?

- I know that start-up environments are notoriously fast paced, and that's something I look forward to, but is top management realistic about goals?

These are the kind of questions you *need* answers to. Some interviewers may not like you asking them, but in the long run, they'll respect you for it. Just remember to keep all questions relevant, and only ask appropriate ones. I know what you *want* to ask:

- How much vacation do I get?
- What's the salary range?
- What are the benefits?
- How about stock options?

I understand that these are important too, but this isn't the time to ask those questions. You have to wait until you receive an offer before they're appropriate. And if you focus on those questions at this stage, you'll jeopardize your chance of *getting* an offer.

What Can I Ask?

Some people advise against asking sensitive questions. I say it depends on what you categorize as *sensitive*.

- If they are going to ask you why you left, or would consider leaving your position, you can certainly ask them why the person who had this position left it.

- If they ask what your expectations are, you can certainly ask what their expectations of you are.

- If they ask why you're interested in the job, ask them what they saw on the resume that made them invite you in for an interview.

The list goes on. I think you're smart enough to figure out what is appropriate and what isn't. If you have any doubts about questions, ask the headhunter or HR representative.

Okay, we're making progress, and you're almost ready for the interview.

Summary of Preparation

I WENT THROUGH MY OWN preparation steps as I wrote this book, keeping track of time. Company research took me about thirty minutes. To be fair, I'm familiar with most of the sites and with doing this kind of research, so let's double that and count it as an hour for most people.

It took me another 45 minutes to research a recent interview team from one of my searches. Again, we'll double that, meaning it might have taken you 1.5 hours.

Add thirty minutes for personal research, one to two hours for preparing questions, and another two hours for practicing. Double the question preparation, but the practicing should be the same amount of time.

When you total it, you've spent about 10 hours.

I know. A lot of you are thinking *I don't have 10 hours*. I understand, but if you want this job, if a career move is important to you, sacrifice something else and spend the time preparing. You can thank me later.

Final Preparation

YOU'RE ON THE LAST LEG of the journey, the home stretch. Before you leave for the interview, we need to review some things. This is an important chapter. Don't skip it. Many items mentioned below may seem trivial, but any one of them could get you disqualified as a serious candidate.

Getting Ready

Dressing: Keep one word in mind—professional. That's the only word to describe how you should dress. Nothing flashy, just a conservative suit (men and women) accompanied by shined shoes and little, if any, jewelry. If you're going casual (do so only if you've been told to by the company), make sure you are "buttoned up." In other words:

Men—Don't show your chest hair. This is not the place to be trying to pick up the ladies; beside, some ladies don't like it. So tuck in those unruly hairs and button up your shirt. Trust me; you'll make it through the day without exposing yourself.

Ladies—Exposing yourself will do you more harm than good. Besides, you don't want the men focusing on *that*; you want them listening to your answers.

Men and Ladies—Please don't wear cologne or perfume. It doesn't cover up odors, and besides, if you didn't bathe that morning, maybe you don't deserve the job. There has *never* been a person who earned a job offer because they wore a certain cologne/perfume. In 30 years of recruiting, I have *never* had a client say, "That person smelled *so good*, we have to hire them." But there probably have been people who didn't get invited back because of it. I know what you're thinking. Yes, I do. You're thinking there is no way a company would eliminate a person because of cologne/perfume. Okay, good point. But let's take a closer look.

First—they'll never *say* that's the reason, but let's face it, people are not perfect. If you've arrived at this stage in life, you know that. People, in fact, can be damned imperfect, to put it nicely. Imagine that one member of the interview team has issues with smells—strong perfume/cologne smells, in particular. And you walk in reeking like a…well, let's just say *reeking*. Will they discount you just because of that? I doubt it. Even *I* have more faith in human nature than that; however, the interview will start on a negative note, and you never want to start that way.

I'm going to end this with a bit of logic, the same logic I used with *objectives* in the resume book. You have *absolutely nothing* to gain by wearing cologne or perfume to an interview, and the smell *may* offend someone. Why take the risk? It's not worth it.

What to Take with You

Notepad and pen/pencil: You'll need something to write with and take notes on. Don't forget these.

Business cards: Bring enough for each member of the interview team, plus some extras in case you meet other people.

Resumes: You need clean professional resumes. Take the same number as business cards, just in case. This brings up another point. I know that headhunters often "fix" resumes before sending them out. In many instances, they do this without consulting you. Make sure this doesn't happen. When you establish the relationship with the headhunter, reach an agreement that if he/she wants to change the resume, they must consult you first. If you agree to the changes, tell them you'll make them yourself and send them a revised copy. That way you'll always know you have the same version of your resume the company does. It is a little disconcerting for you to hand a resume to someone but have it be different from the one the recruiter provided. Remember, you don't want anything breaking the flow of the interview process.

Research: Bring your notes on the company, including the itinerary, notes on the interview team, your contact's phone number, directions to the company, and most important of all, the questions you plan to ask each member of the team.

Be Punctual

Estimate how long it will take to get to the company then allow an extra fifteen minutes, just in case. Then, allow fifteen *more* minutes to be extra safe. What's the worst that can happen—you get there half an hour early? That's better than the alternative. Not much will start your interview day off worse than being late. I don't care what the reason is. There really is *no* excuse for being late. Traffic doesn't cut it as an excuse. Neither does your car breaking down. Or getting into an accident. Or kid problems. Or technology. In fact, nothing excuses your being late unless it's an earthquake—and one the interview team experienced too—or some other natural disaster. If you are the sole survivor of a plane crash and manage to make the interview a few minutes late, that works also—as long as you have blood on your shirt.

Okay, I think you're ready. Get in the car, or taxi, or on your bike, and go. Get to that interview on time.

Don't Wait for Them to Select You—*Show* Them Why They Should

I KNOW A LOT OF YOU are thinking, *If I'm the right person for the job, they'll make me an offer.*

After 30 years of recruiting, I can tell you without question that *nothing* is further from the truth. Companies hire the wrong people all the time. Experts would like you to think that the hiring process is a science, but it's far from it. Hiring is primarily based on the impressions candidates make on the interview team—in other words, it's based on emotions, interpretations, opinions, and nonscientific data. Most interview teams are not qualified to truly judge which candidate is the best fit for the job. They *think* they're qualified—but the rate of failure among new hires proves otherwise.

So if the interview teams aren't prepared to select the right people...

How Do You Convince Them?

By selling yourself as the solution to their problem/need.

But they don't have a problem, you say.

If it's not a problem they have, it's a position they need to fill, and that position has a primary need. Most candidates looking for jobs tend to view the jobs as *opportunities*. You need to get that idea out of your head. The sooner you stop viewing jobs as opportunities, and start viewing them as problems, the sooner you'll figure out how to sell yourself. Remember, companies don't hire people to give them opportunities; they hire people as solutions to a problem or a need they have.

The key to getting the job offer is to *sell* yourself as the solution. To do that properly, you have to figure out what their real need is. You should already know that from the "Identify the Primary Need" chapter. So how do you sell yourself as the solution?

I'm here to help you.

Before you learn how to sell yourself, you need to assess your skills. Earlier we talked about the three most important parts of this book. *Identifying the Primary Need* was the first. The second most important part is *Assessing Your Skills*.

What Are Your Skills?

ASSESSING YOUR SKILLS is the easiest part of the interview process—in theory—but in practice, people often fail miserably. The way to do this best, assuming you have a great resume, is to rely on your resume's accomplishments. Regardless of how you arrive at the answers, the most important part of this process is to be honest with yourself.

I see this problem all the time. It may be more prevalent in writers, but it happens with everyone. Many writers think everything they write is good. When a critical reviewer questions some aspect of their writing, they get upset. The result is that their writing never improves. Don't be like that. Listen to the voice inside your head that tells you where you need to improve, and in case the voice isn't working, listen to other people.

When I submitted my first book to a copy editor I thought she'd have little to do. Ha! I received a Word document from her that was so marked up it was ridiculous. At first, I thought, *Is this lady crazy?* But the more I looked at her corrections, the more I realized I had a *lot* to learn about copy editing. What you're reading here is *after* copy editing. My blog posts are not copy edited, so you'll catch the occasional error.

When you're at work, you are functioning in a *non-copy-edited mode*. Every day. All the time. What that means is your skills *and* your problem areas are obvious to others. Take advantage of this and ask for feedback.

Back to Assessing Skills

How to do it.

Write down your key accomplishments from every position you've held. You should have most of this from when you put your resume together. In a column next to that, write the requirements and responsibilities of the job. You want your answers to be relevant to the right-hand column. If an interviewer asks what your single biggest accomplishment is, cite one that fits with the top requirement of the position, or at least *one* of the top requirements in the right-hand column.

This is not a ten-minute assignment. It will take a long time to go through all of your jobs and list the primary accomplishments for each one, and then make notes about *how* you did each of them. Be prepared to go a lot deeper than the surface, too. You can't just say you have good organizational skills; you have to *show* those skills when an interviewer probes deeper. You may find it enlightening in a number of ways. I've had people tell me that they discovered things about themselves after completing this process. They had never truly realized *how* they got something done until they sat down and thought about it.

A lot of what people do comes naturally, through instinct. It isn't until they analyze, *How did I get that project done on time?* or *How did we fix that design problem?* that they recognize the process they used. Forcing yourself to look at your accomplishments this way often helps you solve future problems.

Your first option is to come up with all the answers yourself, but don't stop there. Use everything you have at your disposal:

- Performance appraisals
- Old bosses
- Co-workers
- Family and friends

How to Look at Yourself Objectively

Suppose you're a program manager, and you just completed a project ahead of schedule and under budget. To assess that accomplishment, you need to ask yourself...

- Who helped you?
- What resources did you have?
- *How* did you get it done early?
- Could you have done it with a different team?
- What skills did you use to accomplish this?
  - Organizational skills
  - Leadership
  - Persuasiveness
- Are those skills transferrable to a different type of job?

Or suppose you're the sales rep who just finished #2 in the country.

- How did you do it?
- How much did your manager support and help you?
- How much of your success was due to the product?
- How much was due to company reputation?
- Can you repeat your success at this new company, with an inferior product and not as much name recognition?
- What skills and/or strengths allowed you to be so successful?

In each scenario, analyze what you did, how you did it, and determine what skills you used to do it. Write this information down for each of your positions and for each major accomplishment.

Another Angle

When you start off on your mission to assess your strengths and skills, it's good to look at what you do, and what you like outside of work.

- If you enjoy doing projects at home and always finish them, that's a transferable skill to project management.

- If you need to get an answer from someone, is your first choice an email, or is it picking up the phone and calling them?

- Do you enjoy playing chess or solving logic problems? Those are particularly good examples of analytical skills.

- Decorating, interior design, artwork and painting all show creativity.

The problem is, companies don't want to hear about your home projects or what you did in college. You must show them how you used skills in your previous positions to solve problems and accomplish things.

When you're looking to transfer from one industry to another, or from one job to another, identifying and knowing how to sell your skills is critical. Whenever possible, you need to show the relevant skills from your work history, but if that doesn't fly, show them skills from anywhere.

Myth or Fact?

OKAY, YOU MADE IT THROUGH the phone screen, you did your research and other preparation, and now you're going for an on-site interview. Before you go, let's review some of the more common myths about interviews.

The interviewer is always prepared. — Unfortunately, that is not always the case. You'll usually find HR and the hiring manager are prepared; in many companies, the rest of the team is a crapshoot. I have been at lunch with managers who admitted they had an interview coming up at 2:00 or 3:00, but they hadn't even read the candidate's resume yet, let alone prepared questions.

The interviewer asks good questions. — Once again, you'll find HR and the hiring manager doing a good job, but many others are not good interviewers and don't ask good questions.

Don't smile too much. — I strongly suggest smiling, though I'd stop short of breaking out into full-fledged laughter.

Don't talk too much. — This saying should be "don't ramble." *Don't talk too much* is a subjective statement. Think of *Goldilocks and the Three Bears.* The porridge was either too hot, too cold, or just right. Talking in an interview is similar. You don't want to talk too much or too little. You want your answers to be just right.

Don't ask too many questions. — Ask as many *appropriate* questions as you want.

Looks and physical appearance matter. — Whether we like to admit it or not, looks *do* matter, and a good-looking, well-groomed candidate will have an edge over anyone who isn't. All the more reason to be better prepared.

A strong handshake can "seal the deal." — I can't imagine a strong handshake actually "sealing the deal," but I can see where a limp handshake may "sour the deal."

You need to look the interviewer in the eye. — Another unfortunate truth. You definitely should be conscious of this and make sure you establish eye contact. Don't stare them down as if you're trying to hypnotize them, but *do* make eye contact, especially when you're responding to a serious question and when they are speaking. You don't want them to get the impression that you're not interested in what they're saying.

Being late will ruin your chances at an offer. — Absolutely true. This one is often a deal killer.

Don't ever talk bad about your former employer. — Another killer.

Don't ever bring up salary. — True. The first interview is never the time to bring up compensation.

If you admit your weakness, it will kill your chances. — Not true. You need to answer this question honestly.

The best person gets the job. — Not necessarily. Far too often, the best person *does not* get the job.

Do's and Don'ts

The Don'ts

I realize a large part of the advice I'm dishing out is "don't do this," or "don't do that." Sometimes I feel like I'm talking to my dog, Briella, telling her "Don't get on the couch. Don't chase the cat. Don't eat the chair." (Yes, she has been known to eat a few chairs.)

Despite all the *don'ts* I've dished out, I'm about to give you a few more to think about before you head out to the interview.

- *Don't* use analogies about sports or too much jargon.
- *Don't* name drop.
- *Don't* answer your cell phone.
- *Don't* talk negatively about *anybody*, not even your ex.
- *Don't* crush the interviewer's hand when you shake it.
- *Don't* ask about compensation.
- *Don't* curse.
- *Don't* be late.
- *Don't* smoke.

- *Don't* walk ahead of the interviewer.
- *Don't* ramble or go off on tangents.
- *Don't* wear cologne/perfume.
- *Don't* wear too much makeup.
- *Don't* drop your guard at lunch and talk about personal things.
- *Don't* reveal anything proprietary.
- *Don't* drink alcohol at lunch/dinner.
- *Don't* take pills in front of anyone.

The Do's

- *Do* bring copies of your resume.
- *Do* bring a notepad and pen.
- *Do* ask questions.
- *Do* hand out business cards to each member of the team.
- *Do* send a thank you note to each member of the team.
- *Do* wash your hands if you use the restroom.
- *Do* bring examples of your work, if applicable.
- *Do* be aware of how you treat everyone.
- *Do* greet everyone with a smile.
- *Do* make eye contact with people.

Review

Let's go over these in detail.

Analogies about sports: Just because *you* like sports doesn't mean everyone does. Besides, sports analogies are often associated with tired old phrases. As far as business jargon—despite what you might think, many people despise business jargon. You're safer not using it.

Don't name drop: Name dropping is associated with…let's just say that if you do it, people will think you're an ass.

Don't answer your cell phone: There are only two reasons to bring your cell phone to an interview:

- If there is a potential for an emergency that you may need to respond to.
- You may need to look up contact information.

If you have a situation falling under the first reason, mention it up front, at every interview, right after getting introduced. Something as simple as: "Great to meet you, Bob. One thing before we start: I need to keep my cell phone on because of a potential emergency at the house."

No need to go into detail describing the potential emergency, and unless they ask, leave it at that. I can't imagine anyone having a problem with this scenario.

If your situation is the second one, leave your phone turned off until the time comes when you need to access the information. If you need frequent access, put it on vibrate and put it in your pocket or briefcase—somewhere it won't be distracting.

Don't talk negatively: It's universally accepted that if a person talks negatively about someone else, they *will* talk the same way about you. It makes you look bad. Don't do it.

Don't crush the interviewer's hand when you shake it: In this day and age, you wouldn't think a handshake would mean much—but it does. Back in the old days, when the Visigoths and Romans fought wars, it was imperative to have a crushing grip meant to instill fear and respect into the enemy. Unfortunately, some candidates still think we're back in those days.

I know a lady in HR—let's call her Rose. She has said that many times, male candidates damn near crush her bones when they shake her hand, and it's usually the bigger ones who squeeze the hardest, as if they have something to prove. Trust me, gentlemen, you don't need to show how strong you are. A respectable, firm handshake is all you need. The perfect handshake is one not too rough and not too wimpy. I like to call it the Goldilocks handshake: it's *just right*. I know you're laughing now, especially you guys. But trust me, if you think about it that way on the day of your interview, when you walk up to shake hands with someone and think, *Goldilocks*, you won't screw up. You may laugh, but you won't shake anyone's hand too hard or too wimpy. You'll do it *just right*.

Don't ask about compensation: I don't hold to the theory that the interview is all about the company, but I do agree with the advice *to not* discuss compensation at the first interview. There should be no need at this point to ask about salary. By now, the company knows what you're earning or what your most recent salary was. If they brought you in for an interview, assume that salary isn't an issue.

Don't curse: A formal business setting is no place for foul language. Nothing else needs to be said. I don't care if it's a man or a woman you're interviewing with, or even a bunch of guys at lunch; don't use any language you wouldn't use in front of your mother or daughter. Remember the professional policy—if you stick to *professional*, you're safe.

Don't be late: As far as being on time, I have to tell you, like my mother told me when I was a kid—if somebody's late, they're not worth a damn. (See the rest in the Final Preparation chapter.)

Don't smoke: I have nothing against tobacco users. I smoked for more than 30 years. But times have changed. Many companies have no-smoking campuses, and even worse, many people have strong opinions against smokers. Abstain for the day. Don't smoke before the interview, at lunch, or on a break. If you prefer to draw a line in the sand, do so at your own risk.

Don't walk ahead of the interviewer: This *misstep* draws an undue amount of ire from HR representatives. (See an earlier mention in the *Mistakes* chapter.) I don't know if they view the move as arrogance or over-confidence, but whatever it is, trust me—it's not worth it. Pay attention by keeping pace with the person you're walking with.

Don't talk too much: This statement needs clarification. You are the one being interviewed, so you should be doing most of the talking. But the *talk too much* part of the statement refers to keeping your responses concise and relevant. In other words, answer each question completely, but don't go off on tangents or ramble about unnecessary things. That's a sure way to lose the interviewer's interest.

Don't wear cologne/perfume: See the Final Preparation chapter.

Don't wear too much makeup: This isn't a grievous error, unless you go completely overboard. To be safe, err on the side of caution, and keep any makeup low key and professional.

Don't drop your guard at lunch: Many companies use the lunch interview as a way to get the candidate to relax. It's amazing how many times candidates *slip up* and say inappropriate things at a lunch or a dinner meeting. And don't *ever* drink alcohol at lunch. At a dinner meeting, you can accept a glass of wine if it's offered, but limit it to one glass, although I still suggest refraining.

Don't take pills in front of anyone: It's not that they'll presume you have a drug problem; they can use drug tests to check that. But taking pills can distract the interviewers and get them off track. As I've mentioned over and over, avoid anything that could take the interviewer away from the interview.

Do take copies of your resume: Don't assume that every interviewer has a copy. Mistakes happen, and they may not have received one. Have a clean copy ready, just in case. (See the rest of the notes in the Final Preparation chapter.)

Do take a notepad and pen: (See notes in the Final Preparation chapter.)

Do ask questions: The company expects you to ask questions. In fact, if you don't ask about the company and the position, you may as well not go to the interview. They will expect you to have done your research and know something about their products and market.

Do hand out business cards: (See notes in the Final Preparation chapter.)

Do send a thank-you note: Put yourself ahead of the game by sending a professional thank you after the interview, and do it immediately. If you're staying overnight afterward, send it from your hotel that evening, or at the latest, the next day. Express your interest in the position/company, and take the opportunity to ask any additional questions or respond to anything you promised to follow up on.

Some people suggest an old-fashioned letter for this purpose, but I think email is fine. In fact, I like it better, because it's immediate. Just make sure the letter is grammatically correct.

Do wash your hands if you use the restroom: I don't think anything else needs to be said.

Do take examples of your work: Some companies ask for presentations or a portfolio of your work. Make certain that anything you bring with you is professional and shows your best effort.

Do be aware of how you treat everyone: This should go without saying. It's really life advice, but it's especially relevant for the interview. Act as if every person you meet could cost you the job, because they could.

An HR person told me about a guy interviewing with their company, a new startup. He seemed like a perfect fit, but on the day of the interview, he was a little too "friendly" with the receptionist. Regardless, she led him to his first interview and said goodbye. Imagine his surprise when, just after lunch, he showed up for the interview to discover that the "receptionist" was the director of HR. She had been filling in at the front desk because the actual receptionist was running late.

A good rule to remember is to never be condescending, flirty, nasty, negative, boastful, or…anything negative. A lot of adjectives can describe a person's behavior. When you interview, you want only one to describe you: professional.

Do greet everyone with a smile: (See the Secret Interview Weapon chapter.)

Do make eye contact with people: This is another one of those ancient traditions people still use to judge others by. It falls into the same category as the firm handshake. I would love to see it go the way of some of the other traditions or myths, but it's not likely to disappear anytime soon. Some experts swear that if a candidate doesn't look you in the eye when they answer you, they're lying or at least can't be trusted. Others are just as vocal in swearing that the idea is garbage.

I don't care what you believe about eye contact; the problem lies in the simple fact that there are different camps of belief, and most people are not professional interviewees. They seek help when faced with the prospect of getting a new job. If they stumble upon a site where an "expert" with a long list of credentials tells them to look people squarely in the eye every time they answer a question…that's what they'll probably do. But if they find another expert's site first, one that strongly suggests such advice is wrong, guess what? Yes, they'll avoid eye contact.

I had a candidate who inadvertently ordered a meal with garlic at lunch and developed a terrible case of bad breath as a result. When he returned to the interview session, despite having chomped on mints, he knew his breath still reeked. As a result, he turned away when answering questions so as not to offend the interviewer. That simple act cost him the job. The interviewer was so adamant over the idea the candidate's refusal to make eye contact was a bad sign that he wouldn't give approval to hire him even though his reference checks showed that this was the best candidate for the position.

The bottom line is that no matter what you believe about eye contact, make sure to connect with the person interviewing you. Maintain eye contact with them for a reasonable period of time. You don't want them making snap judgments and ruling you out for no good reason.

Day of Interview

YOU ARE SITTING IN THE parking lot, and you still have a few minutes to wait. You've reviewed your notes, practiced pronouncing the interviewers' names for the fifth time, and you've thought of a couple of extra questions you may want to ask, depending on how the interview goes. Now get out of the car and earn that job offer. Don't be nervous. The only time for that is if you see a sign hanging above the entrance, reading, "Abandon all hope, ye who enter here."

For those of you not familiar with the phrase, it means you're about to enter Dante's nine circles of hell. And trust me, I've seen some companies where the employees may well prefer any one of those circles to the environment there.

Unless you see that sign above the doorway, you should be ready. Think hard. Is there anything else to do? Anything you're missing? If not, take a deep breath and gather your confidence. It's time to bring out…

Your Secret Interview Weapon

What the hell is a secret interview weapon?

You may be surprised to hear this, but one of your most powerful weapons is your smile. You heard me right—your smile.

I know what you're thinking. *What about my experience? My accomplishments?* Those are certainly important; that's what got you to the interview. But now that you're here, you're competing against people who also have good experience and impressive accomplishments. If you want to come out on top, you need an edge, and your smile could be the edge you need.

A smile has an amazing effect on people.

- Have you ever watched a movie, where the first 30 minutes were slow and full of plot holes? When that happens to me, I start looking for other things wrong with the film.

- How about trudging through the first few chapters of a book and spotting a mistake? Suddenly you find yourself searching for typos or misused words.

- Even vacations aren't immune to the effects. Have you ever been on the way to the beach only to be hit by a thunderstorm?

Things like that put a damper on the rest of your experience. I'm going to let you in on a secret...

Interviews Are No Different

If you walk into the room and shake hands with a member of the team while wearing a frown, or even a serious expression, it may not make them view you with a jaded eye, but it certainly won't give you an edge—and you need every edge you can get, because the competition for good jobs is fierce.

It's a fact that most job offers go to the candidate who interviews best, not to the best candidate for the job. Why not start yourself out with an edge? Smile. There are no defenses for a smile. Once you get the interviewer smiling, you'll be ahead of the pack, and once you're there, it's your job to lose.

A Real Smile Can Be Wonderful

There is a lot of wisdom in old quotations and sayings. One of my favorites is "Laughter is the best medicine." Scientific proof now supports that theory. I've included a few facts about smiling—all scientifically proven—for you to consider.

- Smiling makes you more attractive.
- Smiling makes you feel better.
- Smiling is contagious.
- Smiling relaxes you.
- Smiling is a drug.
- Smiling makes you look better.
- Smiling gives you confidence.
- Smiling lifts your spirits.

Most important of all—when you're smiling, it's almost impossible for the other person *not* to smile back. Even if they don't smile on the outside, they are on the inside. For the purposes of an interview, that's even better.

Now that you know all that a smile can do for you—do it. You can thank me later.

Pain in the Ass Stuff

YOU'VE ARRIVED AT THE interview early, as you should, and you've checked in with the receptionist. She hands you a clipboard with an employment application. Exactly what you *did not* want to see. *They have this information,* you say to yourself. Nonetheless, you take the damn clipboard and plop into a chair. As you fill out the form, you see a hundred different places asking for information you *know* they already have. It was on your resume. It was on your cover letter. You're tempted to skip all of that, or write N/A in the little white space.

Stop

This kind of thing is definitely a pain in the ass. I personally despise this step in the process, and I wish companies would find a way around it. Some do. Some email the forms prior to the interview and ask candidates to bring the forms with them. I would think that in this day and age, someone would develop a program that works with resume-screening software and automatically fill out the basics for candidates invited in. That's neither here nor there. You're sitting in a lobby staring at a clipboard with a gazillion things to fill out.

It is imperative that you are honest on the application. Inaccurate information is grounds for dismissal, so when you reach the spot that asks for dates of previous employment, fill it out with months and years. If they ask for current salary, list it—don't exaggerate or round up, or include bonuses. If they don't give you a place to include bonuses as an option, list your W-2 income for the previous year in the salary box. If you have 99% of a degree, don't list it as a degree. This is *not* a place to fudge on anything. If it asks if you've been arrested, and you have been, put it down. If they ask for your desired salary, put down *negotiable* or *open*, but don't leave it blank.

I dislike applications as much as you do, but suck it up and fill it out. I can't stress enough the importance of being honest. I'm talking *dead honest*. Don't fudge on education, dates, titles, or salary. If you are a serial killer, put it down. You never know; if competition is tough, they may need a serial killer, or at least a hit man.

How They Treat You

YOU'VE INTRODUCED YOURSELF to the receptionist, handed her a business card—and I'm sure you smiled at her—and now you're waiting for someone to take you to the first meeting. After learning about smiles, you won't forget to use that secret weapon, but don't forget to look out for yourself.

What do I mean by that? Remember how we said that the interview is now a two-way street? While you're treating everyone nicely, greeting them with a smile, and acting professionally, also pay attention to how *they're* treating *you*—and others. The company should be on its best behavior today, so if they treat you as if you don't matter now, what do you think the environment will be like later?

It reminds me of an old HR joke.

Heaven or Hell?

A high-level executive died in her sleep. When she woke in the morning, she found herself in heaven, being greeted by God.

"Since you achieved such high status in life, you get a choice," God said. "You get to spend one day in heaven and one in hell. After that, you decide where you want to spend eternity."

The choice seemed easy, but she went along with it. She spent the first day in heaven, lounging around, sleeping, and playing the harp. No worries. The day confirmed what she had envisioned heaven to be.

The next morning, God sent her to hell. She arrived on a beautiful white-sand beach, with perfect weather, wearing a bikini. An old friend of hers handed her a piña colada, and said, "You look fantastic!"

She glanced down at her body and realized it was the best she'd looked in years. Before long, a few other friends joined them, and for the rest of the day, they swam, sunbathed, and drank, enjoying every minute. At the end of the day, Satan took them to a fine restaurant, where they feasted on lobster and steak. Afterward, they spent the night dancing and didn't stop until just before dawn. Before she could say goodbye, she was whisked back to heaven.

"What's your decision?" God asked.

It didn't take long to decide. "Heaven was nice," she said, "but hell...was wonderful. I think I'll go to hell."

"No problem," God said, and she disappeared.

The woman landed barefoot, standing on burning rocks and surrounded by a barren landscape. The friend who had greeted her yesterday was cleaning up shit. Blisters and sores covered his body. The devil came up to her and draped his arm over her shoulder.

"Welcome back."

She stared, eyes agape. "I don't understand. What happened? Where's the beach? Where are the piña coladas? What about the dancing?"

The devil laughed. "Yesterday we were recruiting you; today you're staff."

Bottom Line

Real life isn't quite that bad, but like all good jokes, the ones with a ring of truth are the best. And there is more than a bit of truth in this one, so keep your eyes open and your senses alert. Watch how everyone is treated, not just you. It may give you insight into the company and save you from a bad career move.

First Meeting

JUST AS YOU WERE WONDERING exactly how long fifteen minutes could be, someone came and introduced themselves as Megan Conrad, your first meeting of the day.

What do you talk about as you walk with her? Any kind of pleasant small talk will do.

- Compliment their offices.
- Mention that the trip was pleasant, and/or that the accommodations were nice.
- Tell her how smooth the process has been.

Do not say anything negative.

- Don't discuss how bad traffic was.
- Don't mention anything negative about the flight or weather.
- Don't mention anything that could be construed as a negative comment. People don't like to hear negativity, especially on interview day.

Also, remember to walk *with* her, not ahead of or behind her. Remember to smile. And make sure to show enthusiasm.

The most important thing to remember is that you have no idea what kind of questions you'll get. HR may conduct a behavior-based interview, someone else may use more of a performance-based model, and others may make up questions on the spot. There are a million questions they could ask. Nobody can give you a list of them all, and even if they could, you couldn't practice all of them. The absolute best way to be prepared and stay a step ahead of your competition is to practice being honest. If all of your answers are based on honesty, you should be able to handle anything. Even if you mess up, they'll be able to tell you're being honest, and that will go a long way.

The first step is to know your material, and that should be easy, since your material is *you*. The key to a good interview is being able to cite specifics from your background and make them relevant to the position you're interviewing for.

Strategies

LAST-MINUTE DETAILS are running through your mind. You've made it to the drawbridge, but now that you're here, it feels more like a tightrope, and you're certain that bolts from a crossbow will pierce your armor any minute. Then you remember you're not actually wearing armor, and that there really isn't a castle.

Take a deep breath. I know you may be nervous, but there's no need to be. Picture yourself going in and acing that interview and—smiling. Now that you feel better, here's one last piece of advice. We could review a million things right now, but two important ones stand out.

Don't be afraid to pause.

This is a critical strategy and one you need to not only *not be afraid of* but one you should embrace. Too many candidates rush out a response without thinking and then end up stammering their way through a mediocre answer. When someone asks a question, pause and think. Make sure you understand what they are looking for. If you don't understand, get clarification. If you do understand, think of what you'll say and how you'll say it. The pause might seem like an eternity to you, but nobody will fault you for it. Take a sip of water if you have some and if it makes you feel more comfortable. This isn't *Jeopardy* where you have to be the first one to hit the buzzer. When all the interviews are done and the team is reviewing the candidates, they'll remember how you answered them well, not that doing so took an extra fifteen seconds.

Don't be afraid to say, "I don't know."

We covered this earlier in the preparation section, but it bears repeating. Knowing how to say *I don't know* is crucial to any interview. Some people may be able to get through an entire day of interviews without having to say that, but not many. And the problem is that most people who don't know the answer will try to bluff their way out. Bluffing is a stupid thing to do. It can work in poker, but not in an interview. It's like telling a cop, "Officer, I wasn't speeding," when you know he had a radar gun pointed at you.

If you're hit with a question that you're not sure how to answer, just say so.

"Bob, I'm not sure about that, but I know where to get the answer, and I'll get back to you on Friday. Is that okay?"

Don't worry that you didn't know the answer. Here's why: Even if another candidate was asked the same question and *knew* the answer, you can still come out ahead of the game. *How?*

The interviewer will be impressed that you said, "I don't know," instead of trying to bluff your way through it. The interviewer will also be impressed that you delivered on your promise to get back to him by Friday with the answer. Those couple of days give you time to put together a complete, comprehensive answer that will probably make the other person's answer pale in comparison. The company is smart enough to know that *no one* will have the answer to everything, so you just showed them a valuable skill— several, actually. You were able to find the answer, deliver it on time, and do so in a clear, concise manner. The other candidate didn't get that opportunity; all they got to do is show that they knew the answer to a question.

Bottom Line

I wouldn't say *I don't know* if you really do know, but I wouldn't worry about it if you don't.

Special Note

Assuming you're set up for a full-day interview, you'll be meeting with anywhere from six to possibly nine people. Not all of the interview teams will be strategically prepared with proper questions, so you may be asked the same question many times.

I don't care if you get the same question from five different people—and you may. Make sure your answer is the same each time, because they *will* compare notes. I know of one interview review session where one person mentioned a candidate's response and someone else chimed in and said, "That's not how she answered me," and cited the differences. A third team member laughed and said, "Wait till you hear what she told me." Needless to say, she wasn't hired.

Another thing to be aware of: don't try to control the interview by taking it in a direction *you* want it to go. You *may* have an inexperienced interviewer, and you may be able to take control, but doing so won't help. And remember, you may also have a *very* experienced interviewer who allows you to take control just to see how big of an ass you are. Do that with an experienced person, and you're toast. I know one HR manager who does this on purpose, but a good, well-prepared candidate won't fall for this trap.

Questions They'll Ask You

BEFORE WE GET STARTED with this section, let's talk a little about *how* to answer questions. Yes, (said with a sigh) there *is* a method to everything, especially when dealing with behavioral interviewing questions. Most companies that embrace this interviewing technique look for answers framed a certain way. Some of the common ones are the EAR and STAR techniques. EAR stands for Event, Action, Result. And STAR stands for Situation, Task, Action, Result.

There are other methods, but they all follow the same basic principle: When answering a question, you describe the *event*, tell the interviewer the *action* you took, and then describe the *result*. It's not much different than standard storytelling techniques writers have used for hundreds of years. If it's a mystery novel, someone is killed (event), the detective investigates (action), and then the killer is caught (result).

Forget about any other technique (unless you're already familiar with it) and practice the EAR method. It's the simplest, and it works.

Okay, now let's move ahead with the questions.

Earlier I said no one could tell you every questions they may ask in an interview; however, I can give you a good idea of a few questions you'll likely face in almost any interview, and one of the most common is…

Tell Me About Yourself

This is an almost universal question, but the problem is that you never know *why* they're asking it or what they expect to hear. Many people think the interviewer just wants to hear your answer. Unfortunately, a lot of times this question is asked because the interviewer hasn't reviewed your resume in detail, or they read it three weeks ago and haven't looked at it since, or they read it this morning and glanced over it while drinking their coffee or tea and need to be brought up to speed.

On the other hand, they may be intimately familiar with your resume, and they're waiting for you to say something inconsistent. For all of these reasons, "Tell me about yourself," is an important question. Don't blow it off.

What Do You Say?

This is an opportunity to shine, a chance to rise above the competition. Many candidates use this time to talk about personal things—likes and dislikes, hobbies, children or pets, church activities, sports. Others talk about their education and extracurricular activities. Still others use the time to rehash their resume. Don't do any of that.

As with your resume, this is not the time for personal issues or hobbies, and there is never a time to bring religion into a discussion. Your education and extracurricular activities should be discussed only if they have direct bearing on the position. No need to recite statistics or anything from your resume. They have that in front of them, and they should have reviewed it.

Use this time to *sell* the things not on your resume but that have relevance to the position. Let's assume you're interviewing for a position in project management. Here's a possible answer:

> "All my life, I've been told I'm a people person, which was great, but I never knew what to do with it. When I joined XYZ Co., I started out in customer service. I liked what I did, and I was good at it, but I got a chance to show my

people and organizational skills when I volunteered to head up a fund-raising program for diabetes, and another chance when I organized a walkathon for heart disease. One of the vice presidents was on the committee and was impressed with how smoothly the event ran. Afterwards, she asked if I'd ever considered a position in project management.

"Three months later, I moved to project management and have loved it ever since. In fact, I'd probably still be with them if they hadn't moved operations to New York."

I cited a short response for an example. In an actual interview, you'd expand on the answer. It's normal, and expected, for a candidate to take at least a minute or two to answer this type of question. Before you respond, remember to pause, take time to grasp the question and what they expect as an answer, and only then formulate your response. Most importantly, keep your answer concise and relevant to the position.

Remember, when an interviewer says, "Tell me about yourself," what they really want is for you to give them a reason why they should consider you for this position.

Why Did You Leave Your Last Position?

This question, or one like it, will almost surely be asked at some point during the day. You may be asked it by several, or even all, of the interview team. Assuming you still hold your previous position, they'll likely ask, "Why would you consider leaving?"

There is no *right* way to answer this except to answer honestly. If it was a layoff, say so. If you were fired, tell them. If you quit, there should be a good reason why.

What *not* to say:

- I don't care if Godzilla was your previous boss; *do not* speak badly about them.
- No matter what the company did to its employees, *do not* speak badly about them.
- *Do not* say it was due to salary.

Acceptable answers:

- If you were laid off, say so. If it was a huge layoff, give them specifics. "I was caught in a layoff that affected 35% of employees."

- "Our project was canceled."

- "The company moved to another state."

- "This wasn't the ideal situation I thought it was going to be. I thought customer service would be a good fit for me, but after being on board for a few months, I realized I'd made a mistake. I've talked to my boss about moving into sales, but right now they have nothing open."

Tell Me About Your Most Significant Accomplishment

This question is asked in a *lot* of interviews. I don't know if the majority of interviewers ask it, but enough do to warrant preparing for it. The first thing to know about this question is to understand what they *don't* want to hear.

- They *don't* want you to respond with something from your personal life.

- They *don't* want to know about an accomplishment from college, unless you've recently graduated and have no work history.

- And they *don't* want to know about volunteer work or charity drives or anything like that—again, unless it is relevant to the position.

The *only* thing they're interested in is hearing about your work-related accomplishments.

There is a secret to answering this question that will give you a huge edge over the competition. I think most of us know what we're good at, what problems we've had to overcome, and what conflicts we've had to deal with and resolve, but the secret to answering this question in an interview is to make sure your accomplishment is not just work related, but an accomplishment specifically relevant to the job at hand.

Show them how a major problem you solved—or a conflict you resolved, or a design you came up with—is the answer to a problem similar in their *primary need*. Make sure that your response has direct bearing on the job description. Do that, and you go from being *just another* candidate to being the lead candidate, because they can then visualize you as the person that will solve their problem/fill their need.

What Is Your Greatest Weakness?

This is one question asked in almost every interview, and often asked by more than one person over the course of the day. In my opinion, it is the *most dangerous question*, the one that can ruin the interview all by itself. It's so important that I've dedicated a chapter to this response alone. It follows the Body Language chapter.

Some other common questions:

- What are your strengths?
- How do you deal with conflict?
- Why do you want to work here?
- Tell me about a time you and a co-worker disagreed. How did you handle it?
- Tell me about a time your supervisor asked you to do something you disagreed with. How did you handle that?

You can't prepare for every circumstance; there are far too many questions the interview team can ask. Since most companies use behavioral interview techniques, you can be confident of getting plenty of questions delving into leadership, integrity, conflict resolution, problem solving, analytical skills, attention to detail, teamwork, creativity, and just about anything else you can think of. And that's the whole point—you can't think of them all. But if you prepare properly, and you understand how to respond to *any* question, you'll do fine.

No matter what question they ask, you can handle it. There's nothing magical about any of them. No secrets other than these:

- Know yourself.
- Know the company's problems.
- Know how you can help the company solve their problems.
- Be honest.

Follow that advice, and you'll do great.

Note: A special note about honesty. If you're always honest, you never have to worry about what you said, because the truth never changes. It will be the same in a year or ten years from now.

Lunchtime

YOU'VE MADE IT THROUGH the first part of the day, survived 3 or 4 interviews, and now it's time for lunch. Time to relax, right? Whoa! Easy there. Lunchtime *is not* the time to relax. You still need to be on full alert. All senses functioning at 100% capacity. This is your chance to...

Shine or Die

Far too many people fall prey to the oldest trick in the book. Psychiatrists use it when they ask you to lie on the couch, detectives use it when they bring you coffee or a soda in the interview room, and employers use it when they take you to lunch or dinner. They *want* you to relax. They *want* you to forget you're interviewing for the next hour and let your guard down.

Why do they do this? Because this is where it is *so* easy to wander off topic and say something that could eliminate you. Surprisingly, people fall for it all the time. They say things they shouldn't. Ask questions they shouldn't. And they let some of their less-flattering qualities show.

Common sense should dictate what is off limits, but in case you left your common sense at home, here are a few things that should *never* be discussed, even if the interviewers start the discussion.

- *Never* say anything negative about another company, even if the interviewers say something like, "I know their quality was terrible."

- *Never* say anything negative about your ex-boss.

- *Never* discuss politics.

- *Never* ever, ever discuss religion.

- *Don't* say you want your own business, or that you want to move somewhere else.

- *Don't curse.*

- *Don't drink,* even if they are having a drink.

- *Don't use* tobacco products, again, even if they are.

- *Don't discuss* sensitive personal issues, like divorce or health issues.

- *Don't ever* discuss salary or compensation.

When the company takes you to lunch, be alert. I knew of one company who assigned their top interviewer to all lunch interviews for the sole purpose of exploiting that *relaxed* time with the candidate. This interviewer eliminated more candidates than all the others combined.

Miscellaneous Items

You need to think about a few other things besides being alert:

- You should probably avoid ordering messy foods or foods that could spill onto your shirt.

- Stick to things you can eat with a fork and knife.

- Avoid foods that cause bad breath, like garlic and onions.

- Avoid foods you know upset your stomach.

- Wait for the interviewer to order and follow their lead regarding price range.

That should cover most of it. Now you're ready for the rest of the day.

Body Language

AS I MENTIONED BEFORE, interviewers like to think they are psychologists or detectives, and one of their favorite tricks is to try to determine your life history by observing your body language. A handshake goes from being a standard greeting to a psychological evaluation of how aggressive you are, or how dominant, or how interested you are in the position. Here are some of the traits I've seen/heard attributed to body language in my time as a headhunter:

- Handshakes—dominant, aggressive, submissive, introvert, extrovert...

- Posture—different interpretations for different scenarios.

  - Slouching means sloppy work, or an I-don't-care attitude.

  - Leaning back in chair means not interested or no enthusiasm.

  - Leaning forward means the person is too aggressive, or too interested. (Go figure.)

  - Arms folded—uncomfortable or hiding something.

- Expressiveness with hands—enthusiastic, nervous, person who goes off on tangents, unfocused, excited.

- Fidgeting—nervous, unsure of their position, lying, low self-esteem, anxious.
- Eye contact—This was one of the strongest opinions expressed by interviewers.
  - Too little eye contact—person was lying, avoiding something, hiding something, unsure.
  - Too much eye contact meant—person was aggressive, dominant, overbearing, a serial killer. (Just kidding.)
  - Raised eyebrows—either interested in what is being said, or, doesn't believe what is being said.

These interpretations are not all straight from a psychologist's handbook. Some are right on the money with what the *experts* say, but many aren't. And that's my whole point. Interviewers are *not* experts in psychology. They're not even experts at interviewing. They shouldn't be trying to interpret body language and attributing *any* personality traits to what they see. Interviewers should focus on asking questions and listening to answers.

Why do so many people incorporate body language interpretation into their interview evaluation? Because they think it's the thing to do. They think that to be a good interviewer, you are *supposed* to do it.

Here's my take on it—bullshit! In case you missed that, let me say it again—bullshit! And I say it with extreme confidence. Why? Because even the most vocal supporter of body language interpretation will admit that not all people exhibit the same mannerisms or behavior. In other words, *you* may be a person who leans back when you're comfortable and confident, so that behavior *doesn't* mean you're not interested. You may, or may not, be an expressive person with your hands, which for you may have absolutely *nothing* to do with enthusiasm or lack of it. Your fidgeting doesn't necessarily mean you're nervous. You could simply be one of the *millions* of people who are fidgeters.

Bottom Line

Body language interpretation is the subject for another book, and it doesn't matter anyway. Regardless of what I think, or what anyone else thinks, the interpretation of body language as part of the interview process has become so ingrained in most interview teams that you have to accept the fact and prepare for it, because the interviewers will be watching for telltale signs of…whatever.

So pay attention to your body language. If you're not confident about it, do research and practice the way you'll present yourself. If you do it wrong they may slap handcuffs on you and lock you away…somewhere. Even if they don't go that far, they could very well rule you out as a candidate for the job. I've seen it happen.

The One Question That Can Ruin an Interview

OKAY, YOU'VE SURVIVED LUNCH, you've learned about body language, and now you're back for an afternoon session. Brace yourself, because if you haven't faced it yet, you almost certainly will this afternoon. *Faced what?* you ask. The thing that far too many people dread.

Most HR representatives and headhunters agree on one thing: very few candidates arrive at the interview prepared to answer the one question that is almost always asked. "What is your greatest weakness?"

The question is seldom phrased like that anymore, not in this day and age of political correctness, but however they word it, the response must be the same. The interviewer wants you to tell them what your weakness is, or where you need to improve the most, or where you're not as strong in technical skills or management experience, or *something*.

Candidates get flustered with this question more than any other, and for no good reason.

I'll Let You in on a Secret

Most of the time, the person asking that question doesn't

really want to know the answer. They ask the question because they want to see *how* you answer it.

After listening to responses from thousands of candidates and discussing the issue with dozens of clients, I'm convinced that there is only one way to answer the question, and that is by being…

Honest

Honesty is a much-abused virtue these days. About the only time you see or hear of someone being honest is when they're apologizing for already being caught—such as a politician with his pants down or his hands in the till. After a comment that "slipped" out and offended any number of ethnic groups or religions. Or a more general act of civil disobedience, like drinking and driving. The one thing in common is that the honesty part only surfaces after the guilty party is exposed. People are forgiving souls, though, and if the apology is well written and presented sincerely, all ends well.

Not So in an Interview

You don't get that second chance in an interview. You don't get to rally the troops, have someone write a speech then proffer an apology. In an interview, you're stuck with what slipped out, so you'd better be prepared.

This is not a difficult thing to do. You should know what your greatest weakness is, or as some people like to refer to it, the area you need to improve in the most. People have probably been telling you about it all of your life—parents, spouse, coworkers—and by now, it should have sunk in. If you don't know it, think hard about the term *self-awareness.*

In any case, what it is doesn't matter because that weakness you're about to blurt out is nothing the interviewers haven't heard before. In fact, here's another secret for you—*everyone* has a weakness. Even Superman can be hurt by kryptonite.

The reason you're being interviewed is because the company thinks you may be able to help them solve their problems. They brought you in because of your strengths and accomplishments—accomplishments you achieved even with your weaknesses. All you have to do is show them that you can solve their problems, and you'll stand a good chance of getting the offer. Being honest in this response goes a long way toward earning the offer, because they'll know that if you can be honest about your weaknesses, they can probably trust your other responses. The best advice I can offer is that no matter what your weakness is, be honest about it.

Don't Try To Be Clever

The worst possible response would be to try to pass off a weakness as a strength. I've seen people recommend doing this, and that advice is garbage. If the best answer you can come up with is that you are a perfectionist or that you work too hard, you have far bigger problems than you realize.

So how do I answer the question? You ask.

I won't tell you *how* to answer the question. No one but you can do that. But I'll show you an example of a *normal* response that's a good one.

Let's assume you're a design engineer.

"I have a tendency to rush things. In the past, that resulted in a few quality problems with the finished product. My second boss worked with me on that, and I had to resort to desperate measures to slow myself down. If you walk into my office, you'll see sticky notes all over my computer and desk, with notes that read, 'SLOW DOWN' or 'Double check everything!'

"I also set alarms on my phone that pop up twice a day, reminding me of the same things. When I see these reminders, the message hits home. The good thing is, the process works. The last two products we put out have been finished on time, on budget, and, so far, with no field problems or quality issues. It's actually made me a much better engineer, but, I still need those reminders."

People can relate to this kind of weakness because it *really is* a weakness. The difference is that you've shown how you learned to deal with it.

The good thing about a response like this is that you're being honest, but you're also demonstrating a strength along with the weakness. By showing that you can listen to your boss, take advice, admit a weakness, and then adhere to a rigid program to fix it, you demonstrate strong skills that are invaluable in any number of circumstances.

Preparation

Practice your response to this question so you're comfortable discussing your weakness, but don't make it sound like a rehearsed speech. Also, be prepared for the interviewer to probe deeper. Some interviewers like to dig a little to see if there's any fluctuation in your answer or if you try to back off when pressed.

Bottom Line

Always be honest, even if you think doing so may hurt your chance for an offer, although it probably won't. To summarize, here's what to do when you're asked *the question*.

- State your weakness.
- Let the interviewer know you're aware of it.
- Show them you've figured out how to deal with it.
- Show them that the solution has worked.

If you go into every interview prepared with an honest response to this question, you'll have a better than average shot at getting an offer. Besides, hiding a fault is like a guy holding in their gut on the beach to impress a girl. You can do it for a short while, a *very* short while, but sooner or later, she *will* discover that you have a *belly* rather than a six pack hiding under that T-shirt. And let's not even go to other forms of deception involving swim trunks and pieces of fruit.

Selling the Solution

SELLING YOURSELF AS THE solution to the company's problem is a continual process, and it starts the minute you walk in the door. The process actually starts long before then, but for the sake of this book, we'll call this the beginning. The way you treat the receptionist, the attention to detail you give when filling out the employment application, the enthusiasm you show when greeting each member of the interview team, and the manner in which you conduct yourself throughout the day, answering questions with thoughtful, fluid answers, and asking thought-provoking questions of your own.

But the most important part of selling the solution is how you target your answers, even your questions, specifically on their problems. You can do this because you took the time to discover exactly what their problems are, and then you took the time to assess your own skills and strengths. Now you can bring all of that to play during the interviews.

Scenario One

You're interviewing for a position in operations, and they ask, "Why should we hire you?"

Don't give the standard answer. Quite often a candidate responds with something like this:

Answer #1: I'm looking forward to working here. It will allow me to use my skills and education to help you move to the number two position in the market. I was a top performer at XYZ Company, and I'm confident I can do the job you need to help you achieve your goals.

Answer #2: I'm what you need for this position. I've done it before and I can do it for you. All you need to do is ask my references; they'll tell you what I can do. I am highly motivated and have a track record of delivering and meeting deadlines.

Bullshit Answers

Both of these answers are *bullshit*. Here's some advice. Try not to use, "I can," or "I am" in your answer. And don't ever mention your references. The company will never make it to your references if you don't sell yourself. Companies only use references *after* they've made a decision. They use references to verify that they made the right decision. It's the wrong thing to do, but that's what they do.

I said don't use "I can," or "I am," when giving your response. Why? Because when you use those phrases, it's an *opinion*—and it's *your* opinion. Listen to yourself. *I can do this...* or *I am self-motivated...* Now put yourself in the interviewer's chair. He/she is thinking, *Who says you can do that? Who says you're self-motived?*

You need to *prove* that you're the person to do this job, and the only way to do that is to *show* them. The only way to show it in an interview is with facts.

Specifics

By this time you *know* what their problem is—*if* you've done your homework. Your answer to this question needs to focus on that problem. Zero in on it, drill down on it, and don't stray from it. If they have an issue with low yields in the manufacturing plant, your answer should remind them that you have experience with this *exact* problem, and be *specific* when you talk about it. Example:

"If you remember, at XYZ Company I faced a similar situation. We had a huge sales bump in one of our product lines, but when we ramped up, the yields were unacceptable. I was charged with fixing that. We improved yields from 84% to 98.4% in less than six months."

As soon as you cite the specifics, slam it home by telling them *how* you did it. *That's the key.*

On a resume, they want to know *what* you did. In an interview you need to explain *how* you did it.

Scenario Two

Let's assume you're interviewing for director of sales. Here's a possible answer to the "why should we hire you" question:

"From what I've learned so far, it sounds like you're going through some of the same problems I faced at XYZ Company. I inherited a sales territory that was a mess, and I was charged with getting the team back up to quota.

"During the first few months, I spent time with each of the sales reps, going with them on calls and working on strategy. I got to know the reps, and I also got to know our customers. After six months, I knew where we stood, and I knew how to fix the problems. Unfortunately, I had to let two people go. I brought in three of the other reps in for additional training. I also hired three new senior reps who had a history of being good mentors.

"After the first year, two of the reps we had retrained were ranked in the top ten in the country, and the other one was holding his own. All three of the new reps were in the top ten and had adjusted well to the new environment. The result was that in one year, sales were up 17% over the previous year, and margins were better than ever. And I never had more fun in my life.

"The situation you have reminds me of what I faced when I joined XYZ. It's a challenge I enjoyed there, and I'd love to do it again."

This is the kind of response a company loves to hear. You're telling them you *understand* their problem, you're showing them you've been through it before and fixed it, and lastly, you're expressing interest in doing so again for them. If they believe you, and if your references back you up, you probably have the job. Or at least, the job offer.

Selling by Asking Questions

I'm assuming you've done a good job on researching, and you understand the company's problem. Let's assume you know they have a big project behind schedule, and it's international in scope. The project is a critical program for them. *How do you sell yourself by asking a question?* You frame your questions to sell yourself.

Example:

"In my last position, I led a multimillion-dollar project that resulted in the launch of a blockbuster product for our company. It was a high-profile project that gave me exposure to all levels of the organization and allowed me to work with international clients. I *loved* working on it. If I join your company, what can I expect in terms of this level of exposure?"

A Constant State of Selling

Once you understand their problems and their needs, you have to sell yourself at every opportunity. Let's say you're at lunch with a group, and one of them asks what extracurricular activities you participated in while in college. Maybe you did a lot, and maybe your answer would normally be that you were on the debate club or the chess team, but knowing what you do about this job, you may opt to say that you were the representative for the International Marketing Club and the home-team delegate for helping international students adjust to life in the US. On the other hand, if the position requires heavy analytical skills, you would mention your involvement in the chess club. If it's a sales position bring up the debate club, a clear indicator of persuasiveness.

Think about it. You were active in three different areas at school. Choose the wrong one to talk about, and it does nothing. It won't hurt, but it won't help seal the deal. Choose the right one, however, and you've moved one step closer to an offer. That work with the International Marketing Club, or your involvement with the chess team or the debate club, will carry more than their expected weight when it comes to decision time.

Why?

Because the information was obtained "by accident," or so the interviewer may think, because to them it seems that way. They were simply having a conversation at lunch. Anytime a company uncovers evidence on their own, they treat it differently than a normal response you might give them during an official interview. It's almost like getting a reference. That's the payoff of being observant and alert—and of understanding the company's problems.

Everything hinges on understanding their needs, their *problem.* It is imperative that you know what they're looking for *before* you come to the interview. And even when you think you know, focus your questions and tune your sensors toward confirming what you researched or toward finding what you missed.

Bottom Line

I hope you see by now that the critical job of *selling the solution* is not a one-time, one-place thing. It's a methodical, planned, strategic process that starts the minute you walk in the door. From your first smile at the receptionist, to the way you fill out the employment application, to the way you walk down the hall, shake hands, sit in the chair, and pause before responding to questions. It's reflected in the questions you ask and in how you ask them. *All of it* is critical to your goal.

I'm going to recap the three most important things about interview day. We talked about *identifying the problem, assessing your skills, and selling the solution.* Of the three, the most important is…

All of Them

You can't accomplish any of your goals if you don't execute properly on all three. You need to *identify the problem* to know which skills are important. You need to *assess the skills* to know how to sell yourself. And you need to *sell the solution* to convince the interview team that you're the person who can help them.

Let Me Ask You a Question

MANY CANDIDATES BLOW THIS OFF as *something they need to do,* but they don't attach much importance to it. In my experience from dealing with clients for more than 30 years, this is one of the most important parts of the interview, and many companies weigh their assessment of you based on what questions you ask them. If your questions are standard ones, about sales or product lines or anything else with no depth, they'll assume you didn't take time to do your research. They will attribute that to lack of enthusiasm, or laziness, or both.

But this isn't just a chance to impress the company; it's an opportunity for you to learn a lot more about the company, the job, and the people you may be reporting to and interacting with. It's a chance to draw back the curtains and get a peek at some of the problems and challenges facing the company.

This benefits you in two ways: You receive valuable information, which helps you understand their problems better, which helps you shape your responses better, and that same information will help you decide if you want to join the company should you be given an offer.

Your questions need to show that you did research. That you gave thought to this whole interview thing and didn't just show up so you could fly to San Francisco on their nickel. Example:

suppose it's a disk-drive company you're interviewing with. You've done research and noticed they don't offer a flash drive as an option. You could ask them how they intend to compete in the market when the world seems to be moving to flash drives. That shows you've done research *and* given thought to the position. Ask these types of questions for yourself, too; you don't want to join a sinking ship.

Your Questions

Let's take a look at a few questions you could ask. The focus should be on the company/products or on the position. Make a list of possible questions prior to the interview, and adjust it as the day goes on.

- What will it take to be successful in this position? (All team members.)
- What are the long-term expectations for this position? (Hiring manager and HR.)
- Where has your team fallen short in the past twelve months? (Hiring manager.)
- What did you learn from the last person who held this job? (Hiring manager.)
- What are the three most important challenges for this position? (All team members.)
- Why is this position open? (You could also ask why the last person left.) (Hiring manager and HR.)

Whatever questions you come up with, make sure they aren't simple *waste-your-time* type questions. Discuss market position, how the company lost share and why. Did they have a product recall? If so, what happened? How are they going to counter Company X's new product? A general rule of thumb is *don't ask about anything you can get public information on*. If they're a public company, don't ask about revenues or financials you can find online. Don't ask who the president is, or other officers. And if you do, don't be surprised if they tell you "You can find all of that online."

If the company is a medical one, see if they had any FDA issues. See how they handled the situation. Any product recalls? What do customers think about their products? If it is a consumer-goods company, go online to see what kinds of reviews they receive compared to the competition. This information is always great fodder for interviews, and it's enlightening for you to see how the interviewer stands up to tough questions. Be particularly keen in observing how they answer. Do they blame someone else? Another department? A former employee? The market? Do they acknowledge that there is a problem? Look for recent product launches and note how they were received. Was it launched on time? Were there any field problems?

Right about now, you're probably starting to say, "Shit, this sounds like work." Guess what—it is.

The Tough Questions

We could add hundreds of questions to this list, but let's take time to look at a few of my favorites.

- **What do you expect me to accomplish in the first 6–12 months?**

  - This should get the manager to open up about any fires that need putting out. Whatever needs doing in the first few months is most likely a pain in the manager's ass right now. That's what he/she is going to be concerned about. Show them that you can take care of it and that you're ahead of the game.

- **If you could hire someone who fit the requirements perfectly but wasn't a team player, or someone who fit only some of the requirements and was a team player—who would you hire?**

  - I like asking this question for a few reasons. I can't imagine a hiring manager opting for the *non-team player,* but if they do—run. However, the more important information you want from this question is how they will likely qualify their answer. Most managers will opt for the *team player,* but they'll qualify it by saying

98

that it depends on which requirements the person fits. If they elaborate, you have your definitive answer for what the manager views as the key requirements of the position. If all they say is that it depends, you can probe deeper and ask which requirements they would/could sacrifice.

- **Forget the top three challenges, I need to know what you think is the #1 priority for this role. In other words, if you had me do nothing else, what would you have me start on when I get here?**

  - When you eliminate the flexibility and safety of giving them three or five options, you pin them down on where the *real* trouble is. This is what you *absolutely* need to know if you are expected to be successful. Once you're armed with this information—and assuming you're qualified—you should be able to nail down this interview by showing them you can solve their problem.

Mixing up the Questions

During the preparation phase, you did research on each member of the interview team. Your questions should also be targeted to each member. In other words, you'll be asking the marketing person different questions than what you ask the finance person, or the HR person. If you discovered that the company has a major mission to rebrand themselves and you're interviewing for an engineering role, ask the marketing person how that will affect engineering.

- Will product colors change?
- Will the basic design be dramatically altered?
- How does marketing work with engineering during the concept stage?

Listen carefully as you go through the day. Make sure there are no inconsistencies between what's listed on the job description and what the interview team is telling you. If you see any, make note of it and get clarification. To be successful, you must have a clear understanding of what their needs are; there is no room for misinterpretation or misunderstanding.

Taboo Questions

I always suggest that candidates ask almost any question about the job, appropriate questions about people, but to never ask about salary or benefits or relocation on the first visit. A good rule is that if you think the question could be inappropriate, don't ask it. You can always ask the recruiter about it later, or if the interview proceeds toward an offer, you can ask the HR rep about it then. When I say *salary*, it includes all forms of compensation. Don't ask about vacation, bonuses, stock options…anything.

Now that you learned about the questions to ask, let's move on to the really tough questions.

Asking the Mirror Questions

THIS IS A TRICKY AREA. Many of you won't feel comfortable pushing the envelope this far on a first interview. The safe way would be to take most people's advice and leave the interview in the hands of the interview team. Go along with whatever they have planned and *sell* yourself so well that they bring you back again. It's okay to play their game; there's nothing wrong with that. People have been doing it forever. But…you need to remember that everyone else is playing the same game. Your competition is *selling* themselves and dancing to the same tune. The real question is…

Are You a Tightrope Walker?

If so, continue reading. If not, skip to the next section.

I like a person who pushes back. When I send my books to beta readers, I don't want feedback that says, "great book," or "really liked it." I want people who tell me the truth. "I had issues with your main character," or "the plot was confusing."

When I get beta readers like that, I hang onto them, and I keep going back to them for more feedback. That's how I improve. Good managers are like that too. They take the same approach. They aren't looking for employees who are satisfied with the status quo, or ones who nod and say, "okay." Good managers want to be challenged. They *expect* to be challenged.

If you decide to go this route, it can be the most revealing and rewarding part of the interview, but it can also be the most dangerous. Be warned. It *could* cost you the job offer.

Why Is It Dangerous?

Humans are fragile creatures. Unless you grew up in a large Italian family like mine—where no fault goes unnoticed or unmentioned—you probably have a tendency to conceal your less-desirable traits. The company you're interviewing with is no different, because whoever makes the decisions on what to reveal/ not reveal is human.

What does that mean?

It means that despite what we *like* to think, companies are not always open with candidates. Even if you ask direct questions about their problems, they may hide them. For that reason, be alert for telltale signs of problems. Use common sense. Companies typically reveal what they've been hiding in plain sight.

The questions the company asks may or may not be important. It could be that they follow a template of interview questions for behavioral interviews, and what you're seeing is nothing more than their standard fare. But usually—even when they use a template format—they make adjustments based on the specific opening. That's what you're looking for. Somewhere in those questions, what they're asking are keys to this job.

What do I mean?

Deciphering the Code

Out of all the behavioral questions they could ask, if they choose to ask how you would handle a situation where two of your employees weren't getting along…guess what? Maybe, *just maybe*, two of their employees don't get along. And maybe they work in the department they want you to take over. This isn't necessarily true, but there's a good chance it is.

How to handle it?

If you get this question, fire it back at them. Answer their

Left margin: *Giacomo Giammatteo*

question, making sure to give specifics on how you have handled the problem in the past, then fire back. "You asked about handling conflict with employees. Was that for a reason? Do you have issues in this department?"

You may hit a nerve or two by turning the table on them, but you shouldn't. If they get upset, perhaps you should consider whether you want to work here or not.

Another example:
If the question is, "Tell me about a time when you faced a tight deadline and a product launch that was behind schedule. How did you resolve the problem?"

Guess what?

I think you already know. Chances are that the position they want you to fill is responsible for a project facing a tight deadline, and the launch is behind schedule. I'd bet my last child on it.

Your response needs to get to the meat of the issue. You need to ask exactly when the deadline is and how far behind schedule the project is so you can determine if success is feasible. You don't want to walk into a no-win situation.

What's the Problem with Asking These Questions?

The problem is that you stand a good chance of offending the hiring manager or the HR manager. They *shouldn't* be offended, but you never know how people will react. Some of them view questions like these as stepping over the line or as being too bold.

My feeling is quite the opposite. As I've said before, this is a two-way street now. If they can ask you tough questions, you should be able to ask them the same things.

Now that you're feeling bold and brave, it's time to ask the big one. After the hiring manager or HR manager asks, "What is your biggest weakness?" turn it around on them. If it's the hiring manager asking, take your time, give your response, and a little later in the conversation—when it's appropriate—ask them the same question. It's easy enough to phrase.

"Now that I've bared my soul for you, perhaps you would be kind enough to do the same. If I come to work here, what can I expect to find regarding your weaknesses?"

If it's the HR manager who asks you the weakness question, rephrase it.

"Now that I've bared my soul for you, perhaps you could enlighten me about my potential boss. If I come to work here, what can I expect to find as her/his weakness?"

Limit this question to the hiring manager and/or the HR manager. It would be great to hear the responses from all of the interview team, but that would be pushing the limits of interview etiquette. You could, however, ask them other probing questions that will shed light on what you need to know. I like to ask every member of the interview team this question.

"What is the greatest challenge facing the company in the next two years?"

You may be surprised at the responses. Some companies—the kind you want to work for—will have similar responses across the board. That's a good sign; communication flows open and free, and people are aware of what they face. They know the competition and what they have to do to thrive in the market. If you get a wide variance from the team, that's not as good a sign.

A similar question you should ask is, "Tell me about the challenges facing the person who takes this job."

Again, this is an excellent way to see how the job is viewed by different team members, and you may be surprised at what you can learn from this type of questioning.

Pushing the Envelope

A lot of candidates don't like to push the envelope during an interview. I say, *why not?* Now is the time to find out what problems the company has, what issues you would face in this role, and what obstacles stand in the way of being successful. Once you're on board, it's too late.

If they get upset, you're probably better off not joining the company. If they take offense at you asking a question that can affect your career, what does that tell you about the way they'll treat you when you join the team? Remember the HR joke about hell? As I said, it holds more than a little truth to it.

Don't let a company's success or reputation influence you. Their success in one area doesn't mean they can repeat it in another. A good example for today may be Microsoft. Suppose you were going for an interview to join their mobile team. If it were me, I'd have a *lot* of questions about how they hope to succeed. On the surface, they have a strategy, and they just bought Nokia's devices and services business, but don't take the fluff they throw to the press as an answer. Ask probing questions. Make them show that they have a far deeper plan. Ask how they'll compete with Google and Apple on the systems side and how they'll convince developers to make apps for their platform. Push hard. If they don't admit to their challenges, you probably don't want to go there, and if they do admit to them, they'll respect you for pushing back.

Bottom Line

Plenty of questions you ask could be considered sensitive. If you decide to go this route, make sure your questions are truly appropriate for the position. In my opinion, fair game includes any questions dealing with the job, the hiring manager (within limits), and the company and its products—barring proprietary items.

Assuming they don't throw you out of the office, let's talk about closing the deal.

Closing the Deal

THERE ARE A GAZILLION (I know I keep using that word, but I love it) ways to *close the deal*, and if you read enough articles and books, you're bound to encounter conflicting opinions on how to do it and what the most important thing to do is. My opinion is that they're *all* important, assuming it's good advice. *Closing the deal* should start the moment you walk in the door.

- When you smiled at the receptionist and greeted her kindly—you were closing the deal.

- When you *enthusiastically* introduced yourself to each member of the interview team—you were closing the deal.

- When you gave a firm, Goldilocks handshake—you were closing the deal.

- When you made proper eye contact—you were closing the deal.

- And when you practiced all of the other things we discussed—you were closing the deal.

Most experts refer to closing the deal as the time at the end of the interview when you ask for the job. I agree that it's important and not a difficult thing to do. Some people get nervous about it. Their gut gets tied in knots, and their voice seems to disappear. They usually end up *not* asking for the job. If you find that you're one of those people…

Here's an Option

Don't ask for the job. Not directly. But make sure before you leave that you tell them—with enthusiasm—that you're interested in the position, the company, and, most importantly—in the challenge. You don't have to be pushy. Be sincere. Something as simple as, "I like what you're doing here, and I love the challenge of the job. This is something I've done before, and I'd love to have a chance to do it again."

Some experts insist you have to press for the next step. If you're comfortable doing so, that's fine. But if you're not, just do what I suggested above. Let them know you're interested, show them you're enthusiastic, and remind them you've done this before, and they'll take the next step with you.

Miscellaneous

Before you leave each interview, make sure you have one of their business cards, and that you've given them one of yours. You'll need them to send thank-you notes. If they asked any questions you didn't have the answer for, make sure you clarify what they wanted to know before you leave, and remind them about when you'll get back to them. If a common acquaintance was mentioned during the interview, remind them of that, and, if appropriate, suggest they talk to that person about your background. (Also make a note to yourself to call that person and tell them to expect a call.)

Lastly, give them another good Goldilocks handshake and thank them for their time. Then go home and wait for the offer.

Salary

AS WE'VE DISCUSSED, you shouldn't bring up salary during the interview. If you're dealing with a recruiter, they'll know the range, and they should have told you by now. If you're dealing directly with the company, more than likely, someone has asked what you're currently making, so you'll have to assume salary can be worked out.

But suppose that during the interview, they ask what you expect in salary. Here's a good way to respond. Tell them what you're making and say you'll consider a fair offer after you know more about job/company/challenge. And remember, salary is only one part of an offer.

If they do ask, don't be coy with the company or recruiters. Tell them about your package in detail. A lot of candidates feel that they're underpaid, and they hesitate to say what they're making, because they don't want an offer based on that. Don't play that game. Give them the details and *show* them how you're the solution to their problem. Do that convincingly, and you can negotiate a fair package regardless of what you're currently making.

Negotiating Salary

A trusted headhunter is often quite good at negotiating deals and coming up with a win/win situation. I've seen some *great* HR people, but I can count on one hand the times I've seen hiring managers or candidates who were good at negotiating deals. This is not a knock on someone's ability; it's simply a matter of common sense.

How many offers have *you* negotiated?

Let's assume that you've worked for six different companies, and let's get crazy and assume that you have turned down an offer at another company for each one you accepted. That means you have negotiated 12 offers. **Twelve!** That's not many.

Most hiring managers haven't done many more. But an active headhunter, or a busy HR person, might do 30–50 *per year.*

What Does That Mean?

Like anything else in life, it means that if you're dealing with a competent headhunter or an experienced HR person, they've picked up tricks and ways to do things that a person with less experience doesn't have. It means that there's a much stronger chance of closing the deal if you let the *professionals* do the negotiating.

Side Note

I know what some of you are thinking. Yes, I really do. You're thinking, *I negotiate everything. I can haggle the price of a new car. I can find the best deal on a hotel room. I bought my last TV at 30% below the going rate.*

I understand that, but this is different. Why? Because this is about *you.* And when it's about you, egos get in the way of common sense. What do I mean by that? From the candidate side, here's how many people (not all, but many) look at it. You get the offer, which is lower than you expected. Your first reaction, I don't care who you are, is disappointment. If you let your emotions run with that, it can turn into, *Is that all they think I'm worth?*

The problem with negotiating yourself is the personal conflict. Most candidates forget to look at things objectively. They suddenly think it's all about them. They don't realize that the company has compression problems or internal equity situations.

They don't put themselves in the manager's position as he's thinking, *How am I going to pay the new person, X amount, when everyone else is at Y?*

At the same time, the hiring managers think it's all about them. They start thinking, "All she wants is money. I'm not buying her. If she doesn't want to work here, we'll find somebody else."

The manager doesn't stop to put themselves in the candidate's position or think like they're thinking, *How am I going to pay $800 a month more in mortgage on that small increase in salary, and especially when my spouse will be out of work for months while he/she finds a new position?*

Back to Negotiating

This is where many, and I mean *many* deals fall apart. Most candidates do not know how to negotiate properly, and I hate to say it, but most companies don't either. HR departments often have very good representatives that can handle this, but it's usually a mistake to let the hiring manager be involved directly with negotiations. I know several HR directors who forbid their hiring managers from participating in negotiations. They can be involved with answering questions about technical details of the job or about the potential of the job. They can be involved with *selling* the opportunity, but they should stay out of the financial aspects of the offer.

If you absolutely *must* negotiate yourself, try to do it with the HR person. Make a written list and follow it when discussing the details. Don't respond to anything during the course of live negotiations; instead, wait until you are home or off the phone, and then, after you've had a chance to mull it over, think it through. Don't make any decisions while emotional. You know the old saying, "Don't go grocery shopping when you're hungry"? The same rule applies here. Don't negotiate when you're emotional.

There are two basic levels of negotiating offers: local offers and relocations. The rules below apply universally.

- Don't use the word *if* when negotiating, as in, "If you give me more salary, I'll take the job." *If* you do that, you're setting yourself up for a showdown, so you'd better be prepared to reject the offer if they don't, or can't, agree to your terms.

- Don't draw lines in the sand—for any part of the negotiation. Again, unless you're willing to turn the job down for that reason.

- Don't make unreasonable demands during any part of the negotiation. Example: If the company policy is to allow transport of one car, and you have two cars and a boat, don't ask for all of them.

- Vacation. Depending on the level of the position, companies often have some flexibility on vacation. If you've been getting three weeks, and they're offering two, it's reasonable for you to see if you can get three. It would be unreasonable to ask for four.

- Starting time. Depending on the reasons, this can either be somewhat flexible or not at all. It's not reasonable if you want to delay a month for vacation. It is reasonable if you want to delay a month to get the bonus you're due from the other company. Offer to start earlier if they cover the bonus. Don't be unreasonable on the start date. If you ask for too much time, again, they'll wonder why they offered you the job. If you say your old company just can't do without you, that they need you for a month or more to close down a project, or whatever, you will be showing your immaturity (or naivety).

- Don't get into any arguments over titles. Titles mean nothing, and if you press the issue, you'll make them wonder what motivates you and what's important. In other words, you'll make them reconsider why they're hiring you. On a side note, I've seen senior research fellows making more money and with more influence in company decisions than vice presidents.

For offers that involve relocation:

- Moving expenses. Most of the expenses should be pretty standard, but companies usually have flexibility in temporary living arrangements.

- At higher levels, bridge loans are often available to help in certain circumstances.

- Companies (big companies) seldom have room to negotiate with stock options at all but the highest levels. At the lower levels, they are mostly set in stone.

- If you get into issues dealing with relocation, stock options, long-term equity, or anything else that you're not 100% comfortable with—get help! *Don't* be afraid to ask for help on figuring things out. If you don't know anyone personally, spend a few bucks and get a financial consultant to help you get the details straight so you have the facts to make an intelligent decision.

- Don't use the standard cost of living charts on the Internet to give you an easy answer of what costs will be like. It's unlikely your situation matches their chart. We'll go into detail later on how to use them, and what to use them for, but for now, know that such charts are more trouble than good, and they are often full of misinformation, or at the least, misleading information.

The most important thing to remember when negotiating is that...

It's Not All About Salary

Most people look at the salary and pretty much make up their minds right then and there whether they'll take the job. They may not realize it, but that's what they do. I know. You're saying, "I don't do that." But deep inside, yes, you do. You may not make up your mind entirely based on the salary, but the way you look at the rest of the offer is certainly skewed by it. The positives aren't as positive, and the negatives jump out at you.

You have to start out thinking of this as a *package*. People live on packages, not salaries. Let's take a look at an example compensation package (See table, opposite).

This is how many people look at an offer. Then they figure they'll also have to pay taxes on the increases in salary and bonus, so, at best, they'll be breaking even, if not going into the hole.

The problem is that they don't look at all of the other factors that may affect an offer when relocating is involved.

	Existing	Offer	Difference Per Year
Base Salary	100,000	118,000	+18,000
Bonus	10,000	17,700	+7,700
Mortgage	2,200 month	4,100 month	-22,800
			+2,900

Evaluating an Offer

This is a complicated process, and one you should ask for help with if you're not accustomed to it. Having your accountant or financial advisor take a look at the details, and provide a comprehensive evaluation shouldn't take much time or money.

Let's take the simple table above. One of thing that stands out is the difference in mortgage payment, which I based on a candidate who moved from the Indianapolis area to the San Francisco Bay Area. He moved into a house that cost almost $500,000 more than the one in Indiana, which is why the monthly payments went up so much. At first glance this looks horrible, even compared to the respectable increase in salary. But he had a lot of other things to consider.

Like what?

The mortgage payments amount to almost $23,000 per year, but the bulk of that will be interest, which is tax deductible. Assuming you're in the 25% tax bracket, that savings amounts to about $6,000 per year. Also, think about the equity in the house. Let's assume both houses would increase in value at a rate of 5% per year. After five years, the house in Indianapolis will have increased in value from $300K to $382K. During the same time, the house in the Bay Area will have gone from $800K to $1,021K. That represents an increase of $82k in Indiana versus $221k in San Francisco.

You're also looking at a similar occurrence in the salary and bonus area, though one not as dramatic. Let's look.

If we assume a 5% increase in total base/bonus in each job, here are the results:

	Current Job	New Job	Difference
First Year	$100,000	$135,700	$25,700
After Five Years	$140,000	$173,000	$33,000

As you can see from the chart, you'll earn a little more than $25,000 more in the first year at the new position. By year five, you'll be earning $33,000 more. That alone might not be enough to justify making the move, but there are other factors to consider.

Other Considerations

I've listed some big factors, but there are others. State income tax and sales tax are big ones. In some cases, those alone can make a huge difference. Several states have no income tax, so the difference if you live in Texas (no income tax), and move to Delaware (one of the highest income taxes), would be huge, although Delaware is one of the few states with no *sales* tax. Taxes are something to be weighed when evaluating costs.

Some other items are below:

- Electric (Locations can differ by hundreds of dollars per month. Check it out.)
- General Cost Of Living COL. Although there are plenty of online sites, I'd use the sites that give specific data on items.
- Insurance costs for vehicles and housing.
- Cost of vehicle ownership if your commute is a long one, or the cost of public transportation.
- Private schools or day care, if those are considerations. And don't forget the public school system and their ratings. Many a deal has been made, or soured, because of school systems.

This is by no means a comprehensive list, but it should give you an idea of the scope of factors to consider. And remember, for everything listed here, the reverse is true when moving from a high cost of living to a lower one. We moved one person from Southern California to Texas. For them, it was like hitting the lottery. The $950K housing bill they had in San Diego was now less than $400K in Texas (for a bigger house). They also went from a state with a high income tax to one with no income tax, and they traded a one-hour commute for a fifteen-minute one.

The point is, if you're considering a relocation, first dig deep to consider all of the factors involved. Ask for help if you need to, and by all means, have someone help you look it over.

One More Thing

I've been doing this a long time, more than 30 years. In all of that time, with all of the people I've put in new positions, I can say that it's a rare circumstance when I see a person make a move strictly for the money. Sometimes it starts out that way—or they think it does—but somewhere deep inside, the motivation to *look* at a new position is not money. Quite often the candidate—and that means *you*—doesn't realize the truth, but you're using the money/salary as a justification for the reason you're looking. In reality, there's something else driving you. A challenge. A *need* to do something new. Some *drive* that you may not even recognize.

While you are going through the whole interview process, think about what I've said and see if you can pinpoint your inner desires and needs. The sooner you do, the happier you'll be.

Counteroffers

MANY COMPANIES GO TO extremes once you turn your resigna-
tion in. They pull out all the stops, telling you what great plans
they had for you, how things will improve, about big projects
coming up, promotional possibilities, even raises. Quite often they
bring in the big guns to stroke your ego, directors, vice presidents, executive vice presidents, and if you're deemed important
enough, the CEO.

It's flattering. No one can deny it. And far too often, it works.
But did you ever wonder *why* they waited this long to make these
changes, recognize your contributions, realize you were underpaid? I've got news for you. This wasn't a revelation to them.
They are only doing all of this because they need you, but for
how long? That is the big question.

The Basics of a Counteroffer

Let me tell you how it feels after you've turned in your resig-
nation, reconsidered and then accepted that counteroffer. Listen
closely, because no matter what you think, this is the truth.

Accepting a counteroffer is like catching your spouse cheating
on you. Once that happens, no matter what you might say, the
trust is gone. There will always be lingering doubt. If he/she

is on an extended business trip and you didn't get the call you expected one night…yes, suspicion creeps in. See her/him duck away to respond to a text message—suspicion.

The same thing applies to your employer. Once you take a counteroffer, suspicion takes root. You take time off to spend a special day with your kids—they think you're out interviewing again. Call in sick—same thing. And when it comes time to give that special project to someone, guess what? They may very well opt to give it to someone else, wondering how long you're going to be with them. After all, they don't want the project abandoned midstream.

Bottom Line

If I were your boss, I might be able to toss out all the other things—the suspicion, the disappointment, even the feelings of betrayal. But one thing would still stick in my gut. You *accepted* the other company's offer. You *gave your word* to them. And now you're breaking it. That is the one thing I couldn't live with.

Your company may convince you to stay. They may even give you all that you ask for. But they *may* be doing it because they need you to finish some things or handle a situation. When that's done, they won't need you anymore, and they'll remember you broke your word.

One of my clients called me to look for a replacement two days after they convinced an employee to stay. *Dirty pool?* They're only playing the same game you did.

Before you accept an offer, think hard about it. And if you do accept it—stick with it.

One last thought.

If you accept a counteroffer, you're putting a price on your integrity. What you're saying is, "I'm for sale, and this is how much it costs to buy me."

Misused Words

THERE ARE A LOT OF WORDS that candidates might misuse during the interview and when communicating with the interview team or company representatives. Misusing a word is not usually a deal breaker, but it doesn't hurt to get words right. It's best to be on alert during the entire process: phone conversations, email communication to set up appointments or clarify travel arrangements, emails to discuss follow-up points, or a thank you note. Below, I've listed a few of the most common mistakes. Some of these I took directly from a chapter in my book *No Mistakes Resumes.*

A/an—A mistake I often see is the misuse of the indefinite articles *a* and *an*. The rules are simple, yet people often get them confused.

You use *a* in front of a word beginning with a consonant *sound*, regardless of the spelling. So it would be *a* fox, *a* dog, *a* university (the *u* makes a *y* sound), and yes, it would be *a* historic event. (It is not *istoric*, but *historic*, with an *h* sound.)

Use *an* in front of words beginning with a vowel *sound*, again, regardless of spelling. So it would be *an* elephant, *an* ostrich, *an* antelope, and *an* honor. (In the word *honor*, the *h* is not pronounced.) Words beginning with *h* and *u* seem to be the ones that confuse most people.

Adverse/averse—I have also seen and heard this misused quite often: "I am not adverse to…"

Many people confuse *adverse* and *averse*. The difference is fairly easy to remember. If you are using the word *to* after it, use *averse*.

So if someone writes, "I am not *averse to* rolling up my sleeves and doing hands-on work," they would use *averse to* not *adverse*.

Assure/ensure/insure—these words are frequently found in communication related to job descriptions or in resumes and cover letters. This threesome falls into the *worst-offenders* category. Many people use these words interchangeably, and, according to most grammarians, erroneously. They all have the general meaning of making the outcome of a particular circumstance certain; however, there *are* distinct differences.

I often see statements like this on a resume:

> "*Insured* delivery of products on time and under budget by…"

The proper way to state that would be "*Ensured* delivery…"

To break it down further:

Assure is typically used to *assure* someone/some living thing, of the outcome. Example: You might *assure* your boss that the project will be done on time and under budget.

Ensure is used more for things than people. So to *ensure* the project gets done on time, you hire more people and secure additional resources.

Insure, in its pure form, refers to money or insurance. So I *insured* the project for $10 million dollars in case of accidents.

Here's the easiest way to remember the distinction between these words:

> *Assure* is used for people. (You can make an "*ass*" of yourself if you promise your boss something and don't deliver.)
>
> *Ensure* is used for things.
>
> *Insure* deals with money/insurance.

Alright/all right—Many people think that *alright* is *all right*, but a lot of others disagree, and to those who disagree, using *alright* is like using *ain't*. Why bother when so much is at stake? Use *all right*.

119

Alot/a lot—This is an easy one. *Alot* is *not* a word. It is always *a lot*—two words.

Anxious/eager—Some people use anxious and eager as if they were the same word, with similar meanings. It is becoming more acceptable in common usage (which is a damn shame), but there *are* differences—*meaningful* differences. *Anxious* stems from the word *anxiety*.

Usage examples:

I am *eager* to see my fiancée; she has been away for two weeks. But I am *anxious* about meeting her family.

Notice that *eager* is usually coupled with *to* and *anxious* goes with *about.*

So you wouldn't tell the gatekeeper you are *anxious to* come for an interview. You may actually be *anxious about* interviewing, but tell the gatekeeper you are *eager to* come for an interview. That will mean more to her.

Lead/led—*lead* is the present tense. *Led* is the past tense.

Peeked/Peaked/Piqued —If you're going to use one of these words, make certain you use the right one.

Peeked, is used for things like "He *peeked* around the corner."

Electricity usage *peaked* during August, typically the hottest month in Texas.

My interest was *piqued* by reading an article on the company's new product. (Ah! There's the definition we were searching for.)

Unique—I often see and hear phrases such as *I have a very unique set of skills.*

I hope you know what's wrong with that. Nothing is *very* unique. There are no degrees to unique. Its meaning is absolute. Nothing can be *really* unique, *quite* unique, or *very* unique. Other words fall into this same category: equal, infinite, perfect, complete. Something is either unique, or it isn't. Something is equal, perfect, infinite, complete—or it isn't. It's like being dead. Either you are or you aren't. You can't be *very* dead.

Now that we have dealt with some of the big offenders, let's move on to some other usage problems.

Redundancies

Redundancies clutter writing and make it more difficult to understand. And the business world is full of them. I've included a few of the ones found frequently on resumes or when communicating about interviews. The words in **bold** are the ones *not needed*.

List

- **advance** warning
- add **an additional**
- **And** etc.
- **Brief** summary
- Cancel **out**
- **Completely** eliminated
- Consensus **of opinion**
- **Current** trend
- During **the course of**
- Emergency **situation**
- **End** result
- **Final** outcome
- **Future** plans
- Introduced **a new**
- Join **together**
- **Joint** collaboration
- Later **time**
- Made **out** of
- **Major** breakthrough
- Meet **with each other**
- **Number one** leader in
- Never **before**
- **New** invention
- **Past** experience
- **Past** history
- Period **of time**
- **Personal** opinion
- Present **time**
- **Regular** routine
- Reason **why**
- Start **off** (or **out**)

- **Ultimate** goal
- Undergraduate **student**

Why Does It Matter?

I'm not out to fix the writing in the corporate world; I'd be happy with helping a few people get the jobs they want. I included this chapter because so much of bad writing finds its way into resumes, cover letters, and email communication.

Many of you probably think I'm going overboard on this, that a few words or mistakes won't make any difference. You may be right. Maybe the company you're interviewing with doesn't care about grammar, or mistakes, or anything other than the fit for the job.

Then again, maybe the person who may be your boss does care. And if that's the case, you're out of luck.

A Few Things to Remember

- Don't forget that a phone interview should be treated just like an on-site interview. Be sure you have all of the following:
  - A quiet space
  - A good phone connection
  - Something to drink
  - A note pad and pen
  - A list of questions
- Don't forget the Three P's rule of travel arrangements—be Polite, Precise, and Professional.
- Don't forget to prepare. Nothing makes a good candidate shine more than preparation. Conversely, no amount of talent can help the candidate who doesn't prepare. So remember to do your homework:
  - Company research
  - Employee research
  - Personal research
  - Your questions
  - Your answers

- Don't forget to dress professionally, bring resumes and business cards, and be on time.

- Don't forget the three most important chapters in the book:
  - Identify the Primary Need—I said it earlier, and nothing is as true as this—you must know what the company's needs are to ensure a successful interview.

  - Assess Your Skills—Nothing is so easy, yet so difficult. But few things will give you an edge like this will. Understanding your strengths and weaknesses will not only help with the interview, it will help you in all aspects of life.

  - Sell Yourself as the Solution—I can't stress this enough. You don't have to be a salesperson to sell, but you do have to sell to ensure getting the offer. This is the culmination of all your work. Don't waste it.

And finally...

Don't forget to sign up for my newsletter so you can be alerted about new books and bonus material. Go to my website: http://nomistakes.org

Or

Follow this link: http://eepurl.com/kS-IX

Before You Go

Did I leave something out? Do you still have questions? If there are other things you'd like to see covered, send me an email and let me know: jg@nomistakes.org

If you enjoyed this book, keep an eye out for the next one in the series—*No Mistakes Hiring.* And if you haven't signed up for the newsletter, here's the link, or you can go to the website to sign up. It will keep you up to date on special sales, book announcements, and free items that I give away now and then.

Authors live and die by recommendations to friends, and reviews, so if you have a few minutes, would you consider leaving an honest review on Amazon, Apple, B&N, or Goodreads? It doesn't have to be a five-star review, and it doesn't have to be literary. Just say what you felt about the book. Did it help you? Teach you anything you didn't know before? I know leaving a review is a pain in the ass, but they really help authors.

And if you're interested in mystery/suspense books, check out my other novels. http://giacomogiammatteo.com

Last thing

Remember I mentioned free things if you sign up for the newsletter. Sign up now and check out other articles I've written that give resume tips, networking, how to deal with headhunters… What are you waiting for? http://nomistakes.org

About the Author

Giacomo (Jim) Giammatteo is a head-hunter and has done retained searches in the medical device/diagnostics & bio-tech/pharma industries for 30 years. He successfully completed more than 500 assignments, and he evaluated, edited, and wrote thousands of resumes. Giacomo has also interviewed and done reference checks on more than 1,000 candidates.

As if that wasn't enough to put him into a small room with padded walls, Giacomo is also a bestselling author of several mystery/suspense novels, including: *Murder Takes Time* & *Murder Has Consequences* in the Friendship & Honor series; *A Bullet For Carlos* & *Finding Family* in the Blood Flows South series; and *Necessary Decisions*, in the Redemption series.

His non-fiction work includes *No Mistakes Resumes* & *No Mistakes Interviews* Book I & II of the No Mistakes Careers Series.

In his spare time, Giacomo and his wife run an animal sanctuary with 45 loving *friends*—11 dogs, 1 horse, 6 cats, and 26 pigs. Oh, and one crazy—and very large—wild boar named Dennis who takes walks with Giacomo every day and happens to also be his best buddy.

Now that you've read the book, check out the website. Look around, click some links, and, if you've got time, tell us what you think. Contact Giacomo at jg@nomistakes.org